THE GREAT CAVE RESCUE

The extraordinary story of
the boys football team
trapped in a cave for
18 days

JAMES MASSOLA

DUCKWORTH

This edition first published in the United Kingdom
by Duckworth in 2019

Duckworth Books
1 Golden Court, Richmond
TW10 5AA United Kingdom
www.duckworthbooks.co.uk
For bulk and special sales please contact
info@preludebooks.co.uk

Map by Darian Causby

A catalogue record for this book is available from the British Library

Printed and bound in Great Britain by Clays Ltd, Elcograf S.p.A.

9780715653852

For the tiny one, Sabina. The twins, Carlo and Giacomo.
For those who came before.
For those who should still be here.
For my parents, Carlo and Rose.
And for Karen Jane, most of all.

CONTENTS

'I honestly thought there was zero chance of success.'

DR RICHARD HARRIS

'I can't emphasise enough how dangerous it was for the kids.
It was absolutely life and death.'

CRAIG CHALLEN

THAM LUANG CAVE
Chambers 1–9

Adapted from a map by Martin Ellis

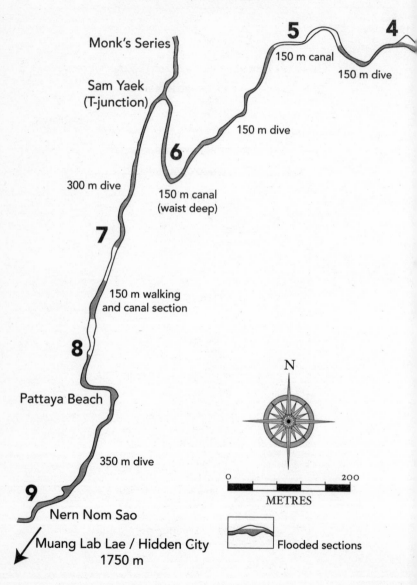

Monk's Series

5

150 m canal

4

150 m dive

Sam Yaek
(T-junction)

150 m dive

6

300 m dive

150 m canal
(waist deep)

7

150 m walking
and canal section

8

Pattaya Beach

350 m dive

9

Nern Nom Sao

Muang Lab Lae / Hidden City
1750 m

N

0   200
METRES

Flooded sections

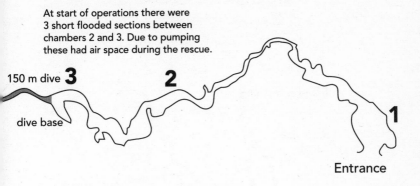

At start of operations there were 3 short flooded sections between chambers 2 and 3. Due to pumping these had air space during the rescue.

150 m dive **3**

dive base

2

1

Entrance

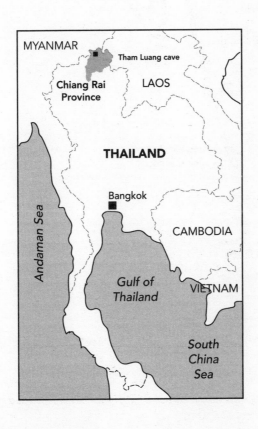

MYANMAR

Tham Luang cave

Chiang Rai Province

LAOS

THAILAND

Bangkok

CAMBODIA

Andaman Sea

Gulf of Thailand

VIETNAM

South China Sea

LIST OF KEY PLAYERS

THE WILD BOARS

Coach Ekapol 'Ek' Chantawong (25)

Mongkol 'Mark' Boonpiam (13)

Somepong 'Pong' Jaiwong (13)

Pornchai 'Tee' Kamluang (16)

Pipat 'Nick' Pho (15)

Duganpet 'Dom' Promtep (13) (captain)

Panumas 'Mick' Sangdee (13)

Adul Sam-on (14)

Peerapat 'Night' Sompiangjai (17)

Prajak 'Note' Sutham (14)

Nattawut 'Tle' Takamrong (14)

Chanin 'Titan' Vibulrungruang (11)

Ekarat 'Bew' Wongsukchan (14)

———

Nopparat 'Nop' Kanthawong (senior coach)

Songpol Kanthawong (13)

Thaweechai Nameng (13)

THE DIVERS

Josh Bratchley (British)

Erik Brown (Canadian)

Dr Craig Challen (Australian)

Robert Harper (British)

Dr Richard Harris (Australian)

Chris Jewell (British)

Ivan Karadzic (Danish)

Jason Mallinson (British)

Mikko Paasi (Finnish)

Claus Rasmussen (Danish)

Ben Reymenants (Belgian)

Connor Roe (British)

Rick Stanton (British)

John Volanthen (British)

Jim Warny (Belgian)

ROYAL THAI ARMY

Dr Pak Loharnshoon

Major General Chalongchai Chaiyakham, Deputy
Commander of the Third Thai Army

THAI NAVY SEALS

Rear Admiral Arpakorn Yuukongkaew, Commander

Captain Anan Surawan

Sergeant Saman Gunan (retired)

LIST OF KEY PLAYERS

THAI OFFICIALS
Prayut Chan-o-cha, Prime Minister of Thailand
Narongsak Osatanakorn, out-going Governor of Chiang Rai
Province and chief of the rescue mission
Weerasak Kowsurat, Minister of Tourism and Sports
Anupong Paochinda, Interior Minister

CAVE EXPERTS
Martin Ellis (British cave expert)
Robert Harper (British)
Kamol 'Lak' Khunngarmkuamdee
Chaiporn Siripornpibul, speleologist with Thailand's Mineral
Resources Department
Vernon Unsworth (British, Thai-based)

THAI VOLUNTEERS
Bird's nest collectors, Koh Libong, Trang Province
Panom Cheunpiron, pump supplier
And a cast of thousands

RESCUE COORDINATORS
Mike Clayton, equipment needs
Gary Mitchell, communications

AUSTRALIA
Divers from the Specialist Response Group, Australian
Federal Police, and the Australian Navy

BRITAIN

Bill Whitehouse, Vice Chairman, British Cave Rescue Council
Emma Porter, Secretary, British Cave Rescue Council

CHINA

Wang Yingjie, leader of a team of rescuers from the Beijing
Peaceland Foundation
Green Boat Emergency

UNITED STATES

Major Charles Hodges, US Mission Commander
Master Sergeant Derek Anderson, Dive Operations
Commander
Search and rescue team from 31st Rescue Squadron
Airmen from the 353rd Special Operations Group

23 JUNE: OUTSIDE
An ordinary day in Mae Sai

June marks the beginning of the rainy season in Mae Sai. The days are long, with twilight beginning soon after 5 am and dusk not arriving until after 7 pm. The sun is at its hottest just after midday but, during the summer months of June, July and August, the heat creeps up on you. Fog and mist, rolling down from the nearby Doi Nang Non mountain range—the Mountain of the Sleeping Lady, in the local tongue—is not uncommon at dawn, fooling unprepared visitors in the early hours of the morning.

If it has rained overnight, a jacket often seems like a good idea during the first couple of hours after sunrise. Mid-mornings are decidedly pleasant, too, as the temperature idles its way through the mid-20s. But it keeps creeping up and, sometime after midday, as the mercury reaches 30°C and the heat and humidity take hold, you're like the proverbial frog in the pot who failed to realise the water was slowly boiling. Suddenly you're sweating, your feet feel trapped in closed-toe shoes and that jacket becomes just an extra item to carry. The heat remains for long stretches of the afternoon and in summer the ever-present threat of rain suffuses the air with moisture; the humidity can rise above 90 per cent.

In this part of the world, you can usually smell the rain before you feel it. The air you breathe becomes a little heavier, its odour somehow a little thicker and—out in the fields and backroads that lead to the Tham Luang Nang Non cave complex—the dirt beneath your feet, which never has quite enough time to dry out, somehow readies for the rain to fall. A few moments before the rain begins the breeze gives the game away, quickening and cooling as it brushes an exposed cheek or arm. A drop or three, then the water descends. If you don't take cover almost immediately, you're soaked through to the bone.

———

Phahonyothin Road, which cuts through the centre of Mae Sai, is neatly divided by a row of well-tended trees and shrubs. Along this main street old and tired two-, three- and four-storey buildings sit side by side. Down side roads and alleyways, the houses are even more modest. Mae Sai is a small town in a neglected northern corner of Thailand's Chiang Rai Province— 850 kilometres from the hustle and bustle of Bangkok, home to the country's political and business elite.

The shop-owners and stallholders on the town's main road are adept at dealing with these downpours of course, but the people on each side of the street tend to handle the rain in a distinctly different way. On the western side, where the stalls, markets and carts are thickest, many of the stallholders band together and run long stretches of plastic sheeting from the shop-front walls to their carts on the road. These market stalls—which sell T-shirts, brightly coloured jewellery, roasted nuts, noodles and an array of local delicacies—are jammed next to each other with no apparent regard for the (probably non-existent) occupational health and safety laws. The sheeting, a temporary affair, is slung so low that it's at decapitation height for anyone approaching 6 feet tall. But for the shoppers who promenade up and down, casting their eyes over the goods, it does offer some protection from sudden downpours.

On the eastern side of the road, shopfronts—home to banks, massage parlours and convenience stores—are more common. There's the occasional fly-by-night stall offering cheap knock-offs of name-brand electrical goods, and more food carts, too. The main obstacles are electrical cables that, every few metres, run across the footpath from the shopfronts and electrical poles to the food stalls.

When the rain hits the eastern side of the street, the pedestrians vanish, food carts are packed up and electrical cables are wound back as quickly as the water descends. But on the western side people barely blink as the plastic awnings become laden with water and pools form under foot.

———

The weather in Mae Sai on Saturday, 23 June 2018, was no different to any other Saturday in summer. It was hot, rain was threatening, and the stallholders and shop-owners along the main street of Mae Sai—typical of country towns the world over—were setting up for a morning of trade.

At the northern end of the street, cars were beginning to line up at the border crossing that leads over the river to Myanmar, to Mae Sai's sister town of Tachileik. The Thai–Myanmar border is a porous one, with people from the local hill tribes who don't quite belong to either nation crossing regularly for work, school and to trade. Identification cards allow them to live in the area, crossing the border as needed, but they are restricted from moving into other parts of Thailand.

On this particular Saturday, the usual mix of local Thai, Burmese and tribespeople were gathering to go one way or the other, while a few westerners on visa runs were looking forward to a day out that would also see their passport stamped.

Decades earlier this area, sitting squarely within the notorious Golden Triangle, was a hot spot for the heroin trade, which has declined since the early 2000s. Tales of the drug trade and, in particular, of former drug kingpin Khun Sa, who surrendered to the Burmese government in the mid-'90s while hanging on to his fortune, still echo through the region. A police roadblock on the main road that heads south out of town to the much larger city of Chiang Rai is a legacy of the area's connection to that drug trade.

Mae Sai is home to about 20,000 people who, along with the 50,000 or so over the border in Tachileik, rely heavily on cross-border trade—both legal and illegal—to fire the local economy.

The town boasts a number of small and medium-sized hotels but there isn't a lot for even the most imaginative tourist to see or do there other than cross the border. If food is your thing, a delicious bowl of Bamee Yunan (egg noodles) with pork will set you back just 40 baht[1] at the food carts and restaurants in and around the main street. Culinary pleasures aside, the town's main tourist attractions are Wats, or Buddhist temples, and a couple of pleasant parks.

But for cavers, Mae Sai is a significant destination. Just a few kilometres from the town centre, on the western side of the road that runs between Mae Sai and Chiang Rai, lies the mountain range of Doi Nang Non. Home to the Tham Luang–Khun Nam Nang Non Forest Park and the Tham Luang Nang Non cave complex, it casts a long shadow over the town.

The Mountain of the Sleeping Lady is a reference to the shape of the mountain and its contours when viewed from afar. And Tham Luang Nang Non, the Cave of the Sleeping Lady, lies deep within the forest park, where it has attracted adventurous kids from the surrounding region since it was first settled.

For thousands of years, the story of the Sleeping Lady, the Princess of Sipsong Panna, has been passed down from generation to generation. Local legend has it that the beautiful Princess fell in love with a stablehand and became pregnant. That angered the Princess's father, so the pair fled. But when the stablehand left their hiding place to find food, he was discovered and killed by the King's soldiers.

Heartbroken, the Princess stabbed herself in the heart with a hairpin, and she and their unborn child died. The water that runs through the cave during the monsoon season is said to be the Princess's blood, and the mountain itself is the dead Princess. Over time, the story has been re-fashioned so that it accords with the Buddhist beliefs of the majority of the locals.

———

Mae Sai doesn't offer much excitement for Western tourists seeking beaches, cocktails and bikinis. But for cave explorers, the Sleeping Lady offers a labyrinth of challenging caverns and tunnels. There are numerous stories of locals becoming lost in the cave complex over the years—for decades it has drawn local teenagers looking for adventure.[2] The challenge of exploring the cave in the dry season, with its choke points, narrow tunnels and spectacular caverns has proven difficult to resist. About 10 kilometres of the cave have been explored, but there is a little asterisk on the south-western point of the current map that only hints at the unexplored path ahead. That asterisk attracts some of the best, most experienced cavers on the planet. But it also serves as a magnet for local kids looking for adventure—like the Wild Boars football team.

The Boars couldn't have missed the warning sign near the entrance of Tham Luang cave. It advises would-be explorers against venturing into the cave during the monsoon season, between July and October, when the huge warren of caves can be hit by flash floods at a moment's notice.

But it was 23 June—a full week or more before July's rains were due to fall. It was hot, and the sky was clear. Besides, in the previous year the first monsoon rains had started halfway through July, three weeks later than usual. Maybe, after finishing soccer practice and then cycling several kilometres to the cave, their blood was up and they just ignored it. Maybe they were driven by the age-old desire to explore the unknown, despite the dangers, the fast-approaching wet season and the difficult passages and narrow pinch points within the caves.

Whatever else the Wild Boars may have thought on that unremarkable Saturday, they were determined to start exploring Tham Luang cave, deep inside the Doi Nang Non mountain that keeps a watchful eye over their small town of Mae Sai. Their decision to enter the cave, unbeknownst to the world, and then to press on and on as the rains fell outside, would prove a fateful one. From the beginning the odds were stacked against the Boars and their coach getting out alive.

The fate of the twelve Boars and their coach captured the attention of the world. Would they escape, against all the odds? And if so, how?

And for Thailand, it was a chance for the nation to come together, regardless of social class or politics. After twelve coups since 1932, the people are accustomed to political upheaval. It's one of the many reasons why Thais hold the royal family and their King, the head of state and a bastion of stability, in such high regard. For Thais, disillusioned so recently by yet another coup that further damaged their faith in the political institutions governing their society, one level below the venerated institution of the Crown, it was an event that would unite them and make them believe in their nation again.

For the people around the world who were transfixed by the team's plight but who had no direct connection to their culture, their home or their people, it offered simply this—the hope of a good news story in an age of uncertainty.

In the end, the rescue was almost like a fairy tale. And it all happened in a cave possessed by a long-dead mythical princess.

———

It began with a Facebook post.

In the days before that fateful Saturday, the young members of the Wild Boars soccer team hatched a plan. They wanted to explore Tham Luang cave, and they asked their 25-year-old coach, Ekapol 'Ek' Chantawong, if he would take them there. Three of them, including Ek and 13-year-old Duganpet 'Dom' Promtep, the team captain, had been some way inside the cave before but, for most of them, the cave remained unexplored territory.

Ek, who was orphaned at a young age and had spent close to a decade as a Buddhist novice, loved his young charges and regularly took them swimming or on bike rides after practice sessions. As a member of the Tai Lue minority, one of several ethnic groups in an area that covers the open borders of Thailand, Myanmar, Laos and China, Ek is one of four members of the Boars who are officially stateless—even though he has spent most of his life in Thailand. After ten years in the monastery, before he achieved the status of full monk, Ek left to take care of his ailing grandmother, who lived across the border in Myanmar.

He first began coaching the Wild Boars back in 2013–14, soon after senior coach Nopparat 'Nop' Kanthawong founded the soccer academy. Coaching the Boars gave Ek another outlet for his energy, perhaps offering him the opportunity to perform the role of father figure for boys who, like him, didn't have much, and satisfying a deeper need that grew from the loss of his own father.

Besides coaching the Boars, Ek worked at the local Wat Phra That Doi Wao temple, arriving after 9 am most days and leaving around 4 pm. According to Phra Kru Sajjadhamakovit, the abbot of the temple, Ek was a clean-living young man who didn't drink or smoke, and who worked at the temple in exchange for board and a small payment. The pattern of his life, the activities into which he threw himself, spoke to the character of a person the Jesuit order would describe as a 'man for others', in the truest sense of the Ignatian order's ideal.

In the years he had been coaching the Wild Boars, Ek had earned the respect and admiration of his young charges as well as their parents and senior coach Nop, who entrusted his young assistant with the boys' welfare; in fact he had hand-picked Ek to look after the younger Boars. The trip to Tham Luang cave, at least in the planning, was no different to previous excursions on which Ek had taken his boys, aged between 11 and 17. But the team hadn't ventured into Tham Luang before.

After some discussion, and a little nagging, Ek had agreed to the outing, posting on Facebook that the Moo Pa—the Thai name for the Wild Boars—would meet at 10 am on Saturday, 23 June, for soccer practice. Afterwards they would hop on their bikes and ride the few kilometres up dusty, broken bitumen roads, past the low-rise farmhouses and fields of fruit, to Tham Luang.

Like all kids, regardless of their culture, the boys conspired to tiptoe around the looming problem of a parental 'no'; most of them chose not to tell their parents what they had planned, in case they were forbidden from joining their friends. The idea was to stay in the cave for about an hour. Contrary to reports at the time, there were no plans for an elaborate birthday party for Night, one of the team members, who was turning 17. They planned to be out by 5 pm, in plenty of time for Night to celebrate his birthday at home that evening with his family, team mates and other friends.

Night missed his birthday party and, more than a week later, 13-year-old Dom would miss his birthday on 3 July, too. But on that Saturday morning, 23 June, all the team members had in mind was a bit of an adventure after a couple of hours of soccer practice. They wanted to see the cave, to explore. According to Belgian-born, Thai-based diver Ben Reymenants, it was a local tradition for young boys to venture deep inside the cave and write their names on the walls.

What could possibly go wrong?

In fact, two team members didn't join them on the journey into the cave. Thaweechai Nameng, 13, had obeyed his parents and returned home after practice to finish his homework. Songpol Kanthawong, also 13, didn't want to explore the cave; he didn't ride his bike to practice that day, and was picked up by one of his parents afterwards. It was a fateful decision that, hours later, when the alarm was first raised at 6 pm, would lead to the discovery of a crucial piece of information.

———

Coach Ek isn't the only stateless member of the Wild Boars soccer team. Three of the boys—Adul Sam-on, 14; Pornchai 'Tee' Kamluang, 16; and Mongkol 'Mark' Boonpiam, 13—are caught in a similar legal limbo. It is not uncommon. The UN High Commission for Refugees has estimated there are as many as 480,000 stateless people living in Thailand.

While the distance between the town of Mae Sai, Thailand, and Tachileik, Myanmar—separated by a river with two border crossings, and which can be waded by the adventurous—can be measured in only metres, the cultural gap between these two neighbouring countries is great. For all its recent history of coups and political instability, Thailand is a relatively prosperous country compared to Myanmar: about 35 million tourists visit the country each year, its manufacturing and services sectors are growing, and the average annual wage is around 165,000 baht.[3] It may not sound like much by Western standards, but when the cost of living is very low, it is enough.

Myanmar, in comparison, relies heavily on agriculture to drive its economy. The repressive military junta still appoints a quarter of the parliament despite all the 'progress' towards democracy; journalists are arrested for doing their jobs; and Myanmar has an appalling history of mistreating the ethnic Rohingya Muslim minority who live near its border with Bangladesh. In August 2018 the United Nations accused the Myanmar military of committing genocide the previous year.

In other words, Myanmar's quality of living is years behind Thailand's. And even though daily staples are even cheaper in Myanmar, Thais earn on average about three times as much as their neighbours. About a quarter of Myanmar's citizens live below the poverty line, compared to about 7 per cent of Thais.

The people of Mae Sai are nowhere near as rich as the political and economic elite in Bangkok but, unlike their near neighbours in Tachileik, they have access to opportunity and affluence.

———

Neither Thailand nor Myanmar offers citizenship by birth, but the porous border has allowed people like the four stateless Wild Boars to seek opportunities, such as a better education, in Thailand.

Adul Sam-on is a classic case in point. The only Christian member of the team, Adul was born in Myanmar, but when he was 6 his family slipped him across the border so he could attend the local Ban Wiang Phan school in Mae Sai. Soon after arriving in Thailand, the now eighth-grader was taken into the care of the Mae Sai Grace church and he has since excelled in the classroom and on the sporting field, winning friends along the way.

The Mae Sai Grace church, situated in a back street off the Phahonyothin Road that runs into the centre of town, is dirt poor. It's not much more than a handful of buildings, including the church and a separate building that offers humble accommodation. White paint peels off the walls, ageing play equipment sits in the front yard and chickens roam around free.

Adul speaks Thai, Burmese, English, Chinese and Wa—the language of the ethnic tribal group from which he is descended; these language skills would prove invaluable to the Boars in the days to come.

As with Ek and Adul, Mark and Tee's statelessness didn't matter to the other Wild Boars; they would enter the Tham Luang cave as a team. Their families would suffer in the same way while, for eighteen days, the world watched, waited and hoped.

23 JUNE: INSIDE
A rising sense of dread

The entrance to Tham Luang cave bristles with promise for young explorers seeking adventure. Outside the signs highlight points of interest, with some of the chambers given evocative names such as 'Hidden City', 'Maze City', 'Stalactite Cave' and 'the Planetarium'. The lure of secret caves—spectacular caverns with stalactites hanging low from the ceiling and stalagmites pushing up from the floor—can be difficult to resist, in spite of the warning sign at the entrance. Inside, more than 10 kilometres of tunnels, the only section of the cave that has been explored, beckon; its full extent is not known. Cave surveys can be like treasure maps, with sections marked simply 'unexplored', luring cavers with a lust to explore the unknown.

If anything, the prospect of a little danger was a magnet that drew the Wild Boars into Tham Luang rather than scared them away. The dark caverns, slippery rocks, pinch points and wide open chambers offered an other-worldly experience, an adventure free of the expectations of their school teachers and parents.

When the Wild Boars arrived at the entrance that Saturday afternoon, they parked their bikes against a railing. A little further in, they set aside their shoes and backpacks, which would later be found by the rescue workers frantically searching for them.

Coach Ek thought he had come prepared. He had ventured into the cave before, along with two members of his team, so this time he had packed a rope, a torch and some spare batteries to help guide the boys deep inside the network of tunnels and caverns.

The further you travel into Tham Luang, the harder it is to cope with the dark. As the 35-year-old Canadian diver Erik Brown, who would spend days deep inside the cave during the rescue effort, put it: 'When people are afraid of the dark, inside a cave is the darkest place on the planet. You don't want to be there. You are 3 kilometres from light. There is just zero light, there is nothing.'

And there are other dangers arising from sensory deprivation. The further in you go, the harder it is to hear anything outside. Later the boys would say they thought they had heard chickens, dogs barking and helicopters from their vantage point deep inside the cave. But it's not clear how this was possible, given the team was hundreds of metres beneath the surface.

But Adul would later say that hearing those noises 'boosted our morale a lot. It gave us hope that there were someone searching for us.'

And Ek said: 'When I heard the noise on the first night, I was sure that someone would come and help us. I told the kids that we had to survive until someone found us. It was only a matter of time. Personally, I didn't think it'd take too long— I only thought it would be about three days.'

With hindsight, the decision not to take food and water with them looks like an obvious mistake but, at the time, the group had not expected to be in the cave for more than an hour—their parents wouldn't even notice they had gone.

———

Those first steps into the cave went smoothly enough for the Boars. When it's dry, the 1-kilometre walk from the cave entrance to what the rescue teams later dubbed chamber 3 is smooth enough, although diver Brown says there are some 'gnarly bits'. As you walk in from the outside world, you encounter one of those sections just before the entrance to chamber 3. Danish diver Ivan Karadzic, who would later work alongside Brown and play a key role in the rescue, says there is 'a small restriction' there. Days after the boys entered the system—well after the rain had hit—that section of the cave became fully submerged; to enter chamber 3, you had to dive about 5 metres through a sump, a section of a cave that is underwater.

On that Saturday afternoon, as the boys walked deeper and deeper into Tham Luang, searching for hidden cities and adventure, that choke point was clear. But a little more than an hour later, all that would change, with potentially tragic consequences.

Deeper and deeper into the cave they went, making their way through pinch points so narrow they could be measured in just centimetres, and then on through the caverns. At certain points the ceilings of the warren of caves and passages are less than a metre high; at others, they can be as high as 10 metres.

Perhaps they felt like Frodo Baggins in Tolkien's *The Hobbit*, making their way through the goblin caves of the Misty Mountain. Some, like 11-year-old Chanin 'Titan' Vibulrungruang and 13-year-old Somepong 'Pong' Jaiwong, would later remember that they were more than a little scared about their journey into the cave, but the promise of adventure conquered their fear and drew them in.

Outside, the monsoon rains began to fall . . .

———

Unless you've experienced a monsoonal downpour in the open air, it's hard to understand just how ferocious it can be. First, it's the air you breathe—one minute it's sticky and hot and the mercury is hovering somewhere above 30°C, the next the air you suck into your lungs becomes a little cooler and more comfortable; in fact it's quite refreshing, but that sensation doesn't last long.

Then you notice that everything is turning grey as clouds gather rapidly overhead. That can happen quickly—in five or ten minutes. Then it's as if, high above, a switch has been flicked. The first few drops, slow and heavy, land on your head, tickling your arm and splattering on the ground.

But a minute later the laden clouds dump thick, heavy globules of water all over you as the rain thumps into the ground. Everything is soaked in an instant. The rain can seem inexhaustible, beating down beyond all rhyme and reason for hours at a time.

But deep inside Tham Luang on Saturday, 23 June, the Wild Boars missed Mother Nature's warning signs. They saw, heard and felt nothing. And although they didn't know it yet, they were already trapped inside the cave.

———

Once the monsoonal rain started, water began pouring into the cave from nearby streams close to the entrance, and through barely perceptible cracks and crevices hundreds of metres above them.

As the boys made their way into the cave, they encountered some water at a difficult to traverse T-junction, known as Sam Yaek, which sits further into the cave, about 750 metres past chamber 3. If they had turned right, the boys would have headed towards Monk's Series, where searchers would later attempt to drill down into the cave, but water was already entering the cave from that direction, blocking their way. Instead, they turned left and headed towards a spot locals have nicknamed Pattaya Beach, after a Thai resort town more than 1000 kilometres south. Ek wasn't concerned about the water at the T-junction, as there had been some water there when he had last visited the cave.

It would turn out to be a monumental mistake.

The boys kept hiking deeper into the cave, past Pattaya Beach towards Nern Nom Sao, another point that offered high ground. Time was getting away from them, as tends to happen when boys go exploring. Ek reminded the boys that they could spend no more than an hour exploring the cave, and then they would have to head straight out, as Night had to be home for his birthday and Titan had an appointment with a tutor at home at 5 pm that afternoon.

They still didn't realise the danger they were in.

When they reached Nern Nom Sao, the boys stopped again to discuss whether they should keep going deeper into the cave.

They pressed on.

It wasn't until they were well past Nern Nom Sao—the place that would become their home for more than two weeks— that the boys realised they were out of time. As Ek recalled, 'When we were trying to come out, we were beyond Nern Nom Sao . . . I'm not sure what the place's name is, but we found out it is called Muang Lab Lae.' The literal translation of Muang Lab Lae is 'underwater world'.

Tee had volunteered to be a scout and had swum ahead through a watery section, and reassured the boys it was safe to proceed.

As Tee swam in the direction of Muang Lab Lae, he reassured the group the water wasn't deep. The older boys offered the younger, smaller members of the group piggybacks—all of them could swim, contrary to what had been reported when the boys were trapped, but not all were good swimmers.

But then Ek checked his watch on their way across, and realised the time. The hour inside the cave had passed quickly, and it was time to turn back and head out. The boys agreed they would come back and explore the cave another time. But as they began the trek back through the caverns and tunnels of Tham Luang cave, the water levels deep inside the Mountain of the Sleeping Lady were rising. Only now, as they made their way towards the entrance, did the Boars begin to realise how much trouble they might be in.

As they arrived at the T-junction, 14-year-old Ekarat 'Bew' Wongsukchan let out a shout: 'The way out is blocked!'

'Are we lost?' another boy asked.

Panic was now beginning to set in among some of the younger members of the team. They were still more than a kilometre from the cave entrance—they hadn't even reached chamber 3 yet—and the floodwaters were rising around them. Mark worried they wouldn't get out and that his mother would scold him for being home late. Ek reassured his young charges they weren't lost, because at that point there was only one way in and out of the cave.

Increasingly wary of the dangers that might lie ahead, the coach gathered some of the older boys—Tee, Adul and Night—and told them he had a plan. Carefully unfurling the rope he had brought with him, Ek explained he would swim ahead and try to assess the conditions. He told the trio to hold tight onto the rope: two yanks on the rope meant danger ahead and they were to pull him back to safety; however, if the rope remained slack, that meant he had managed to swim through the choke point, and the other boys would be able to follow him.

Ek then lowered himself into the water and started swimming but it was, as he later recalled, 'all sand and rock . . . I wasn't able to do anything more.' He couldn't make any headway through the rising waters.

With a heavy heart he pulled twice on the rope and his three young charges helped him back to shore. 'I told them we could not go home; we will have to find another way out.'

They were trapped.

The team frantically started digging as Ek thought it might reduce the water levels at the T-junction, but it made no difference. An hour later, as 6 pm came and went and the boys began to tire, Tee turned to Ek and said plainly the team needed to find a place to sleep for the night. The boys had no food, no water and no spare clothes; they were wet, and a long night in the cave with no dinner stretched ahead of them.

So the Boars turned and headed back inside the cave, seeking higher ground about 200 metres past the T-junction as the waters around them began to rise. Here water dripped from the ceiling, and Ek told them it was safer to be near a water source. The young coach thought the rising water in the cave was temporary, caused by a little early rain, and they could go home the next morning. How wrong he was.

Thankfully, in those crucial first hours after the team became trapped, Ek realised fear could be one of the biggest dangers facing the boys. So before they went to sleep, the former Buddhist monk guided them in prayers he had spent years reciting in the local monastery. He wasn't scared, or at least he didn't let on that he was; he composed himself. As he would later recount to a journalist, 'I did not tell them that we were stuck in the cave. I just told them in a positive way, like, just wait for a while, the water may decrease and then we can get out. I tried not to freak them out. If I had told them that we were stuck in the cave they would have freaked out.'[1]

———

Time slows down in the dark. As the hours tick by, it becomes harder and harder to keep track of day and night. Tee would regularly check his watch, providing the team with updates and trying to provide the Boars with an anchor point in time as the dark settled around them.

Outside, although they didn't know it, the rains continued to beat down. Inside, illuminated by the torch light they were carefully conserving, the water levels continued to rise, and the boys were forced to seek out higher ground. Soon enough they found themselves retracing their steps, heading past Pattaya Beach to Nern Nom Sao, further into the cave complex and further away from help.

Ek told his young charges to drink the water that dripped down from the stalactites hanging from the roof. Filtered by the ground above, it tasted fine, but it was a poor substitute for food; it filled their stomachs, but didn't satisfy them.

Hours, and then days, ticked by, with no sign of rescue. Was anyone coming to get them?

23–25 JUNE: OUTSIDE
Sound the alarm

During the first hours of the search Songpol Kanthawong's decision not to join his team mates in the cave would prove critical. He and his team mate Thaweechai Nameng, along with the rest of the world, would end up watching as a massive rescue operation was mounted to save their young team mates.

It wasn't until about 6 pm, when the boys inside the cave were scampering towards higher ground, that Kanthawong's uncle, Nopparat 'Nop' Kanthawong, checked his phone for the first time in hours. There were more than a dozen missed calls from concerned parents.

He started ringing around to the missing members of the team, trying to find out what had happened to them. Eventually his nephew put him on the right track. The team had gone to the cave after practice earlier in the day, young Songpol told his uncle. Nop started to spread the word that they were missing.

Coach Nop, as he is affectionately known, has worked at the Wild Boars Academy for nearly five years. His own under-19 Boars team had a game at 7 pm that night. After it ended, Nop looked for the missing boys at the Boars' training ground, which is not much more than a couple of ovals overlooked by a small, tired old grandstand.

When there was still no sign of them, Nop didn't hesitate. He went straight to the cave, taking the parents of two of the boys with him. Fortuitously, on the road to the cave, the three of them ran into some Thai soldiers, who accompanied them to the entrance, where forest rangers were already in possession of the bags and bikes the boys had left behind. The parents recognised their sons' belongings. There was no doubt about it anymore—the boys were in Tham Luang, either lost or trapped.

Nop called Go Lhong, the president of Wild Boars Academy and the headman of the village in the Tham Luang area. Luckily a village meeting was underway and some senior local government officials came down to the cave as quickly as they could.

Two local officials, two forest rangers and two soldiers then headed into the cave. They were the first search party to head into the cave to look for the boys, at 9 pm on the Saturday evening. As the world would learn in the days and weeks to come, they were woefully underprepared.

That first six-person search team emerged from the cave around midnight. Floodwater had prevented them from going any further than the T-junction. According to a member of this search party, the sound of the water surging through the tunnels and caverns of the cave was so loud it was terrifying. They couldn't know it at the time but the boys and coach Ek were only a few hundred metres away, on the other side of the T-junction.

Outside, even as the driving rain continued to fall, a second team of rescuers arrived. They too were able to make little progress as they were neither rescue divers, nor equipped for getting through such confined spaces.

At midnight, Narongsak Osatanakorn, the Governor of Chiang Rai Province, was notified that a group of boys was missing at Tham Luang. By 2 am, as those first fumbling rescue efforts were underway, he was at the cave. At first, Narongsak thought it was 'just a normal case of missing children'; little did he know just how difficult this rescue would prove to be. A hands-on technocrat, he would become the face of the rescue effort in the days and weeks ahead, briefing the world—even after he was supposed to have commenced his governorship of another province.

At the cave entrance, Narongsak found some of the parents crying, pleading with rescue workers to get their boys out. But the first responders were forced to admit they couldn't reach the boys, trapped as they were past the T-junction. A third rescue team was sent in soon afterwards but the water levels were now rising so rapidly that they returned in about 80 minutes—they couldn't even reach the T-junction, and water was now seeping into chamber 1, the closest to the entrance.

Five dive rescue teams were then called in from nearby Chiang Rai, and another from Chiang Mai. Narongsak also summoned a team of Thai Navy SEALs, who would enter the cave for the first time early on Monday morning and play a key role in the rescue.

———

About 2 am on Sunday morning, less than twelve hours after the boys went missing, a call was made to Vernon Unsworth, a 63-year-old British cave enthusiast who for much of the year lives in nearby Chiang Rai, asking him to come down to the cave and help. About four hours later, he in turn called his friend, Kamol Khunngarmkuamdee, otherwise known as Mr Lak, a former ranger in the Tham Luang–Khun Nam Nang Non Forest Park as well as a security guard at the Mae Sai Prasitsart school, which six of the Wild Boars attend. His boss at the forest park had already informed Lak about the missing boys but as soon as Unsworth called him, he knew they must be in serious trouble.

For six years Unsworth and Lak had explored the caves and the surrounding park on long weekly hikes together. At first they were accompanied by a colleague, but after three months he dropped out. As Lak tells it, the pair developed a firm friendship on those long, exploratory walks as well as a detailed knowledge of the local topography that would be invaluable in the early days of the search for the Boars. Although neither man has any expertise in cave diving, both are expert cave explorers; in fact, Unsworth has 40 years' experience under his belt.

The two men hoped the team would have found dry ground in the Pattaya Beach chamber, about 2 kilometres into the cave. When the boys were eventually found, they couldn't believe they had reached Nern Nom Sao, 2.25 kilometres from the entrance, which came to be known as chamber 9.

After the boys went missing, Lak spent every day at the cave helping out wherever he could. 'I don't care about anything except their safety, I just keep focusing on the kids. I can't help search for them [in the cave] but I [do] all I can to support and talk to their parents. I try to make them feel better by encouraging them,' he recalls.

Unsworth had been planning his own expedition for that Sunday morning, 24 June; with the cut-off point for the rainy season, 1 July, fast approaching, he had wanted to see what the water levels in the cave network were like.[1] Instead, he and Lak teamed up in the early hours of Sunday, 24 June, outside the cave, for a very different type of expedition.

They had no idea what awaited them.

————

On the morning of Sunday, 24 June, while the rescue efforts began to ramp up outside the cave, the parents of the Wild Boars were growing increasingly frantic. Where were their boys? Helpless, they gathered outside the cave, hoping for a scrap of good news as the hours began to stretch before them. Those early days were some of the hardest; with the waters rising and the rain still thundering down, there was little they could do but wait.

Kiang Kamluang learnt her 16-year-old son Tee was missing somewhere in the cave at about 1 am on Sunday morning: 'His friend came and told us that Tee was trapped in the cave. He told me not to worry as they tried to help but there was a lot of water, and we had to wait. I couldn't sleep.

'Tee's dad was working on the other side [over the border in Myanmar]. In the morning, he came back so Tee's dad and I rushed to the cave.'

She sums up her feelings in those early days, when the boys were lost, with one word—'hopeless'. 'I cried a lot every day. I couldn't sleep well—I always woke up after 1 hour.'

Many of the parents, including Mrs Kamluang, a domestic worker, stopped work while their boys were trapped inside the cave. Wracked by fear and anxiety, they would instead gather at what became known as the base camp of the operation, carefully separated from the hungry international press, who were constantly on high alert for any tidbit of news. The local community rallied to their cause, making donations of 500 to 1000 baht so these families would have some money for daily expenses while they had no income.[2] Every little bit helped. The donations were just one manifestation of the many ways the Mae Sai community, and Thais more broadly, pulled together to help as the fate of the boys and their coach hung in the balance.

Most of the time, Mrs Kamluang—unable to do much else—would simply pray for her son's safety. Implying that at times she feared the worst, she says now that she 'just wanted to see him, whatever [his] condition. I did consult a medium who said that my son was safe. I made an offering to build a bamboo structure [a kind of spirit house] if Tee was to return safely. So, I built it with his dad and we placed it in front of the cave.'

Namhom Boonpiam, the mother of 13-year-old 'Mark', was, if anything, in a worse state than Mrs Kamluang. She would wait outside the cave each day for news of her son's rescue. Sometimes it simply became too much for her: 'I went to hospital three times because I often fainted. I was weak. I hardly ate and couldn't sleep at night,' she remembers.

In the weeks ahead, the parents and other relatives of the boys would never break their long, lonely vigil outside the cave, waiting and hoping for good news about their sons. As the rain fell, day after day, and as rescue workers tried to find a way into the cave, there was no guarantee the parents would ever see their sons again.

———

News of the missing boys was filtering out by word of mouth into the wider Mae Sai community. The first local and international media reports were also emerging, about a team of boys lost in a far-flung cave complex that few people beyond northern Thailand had ever heard of. Outside the Tham Luang cave, the rescue effort was ramping up. But few would have anticipated that, in the days and weeks ahead, the saga of the Thai soccer team would capture the attention of the world.

While the first groups of local divers, forest park rangers and then Thai Navy SEALs began to assemble on site at Tham Luang to plot the rescue, Unsworth and Lak also arrived. It may not have been apparent at the time, but their contribution in those early days of the rescue effort was crucial, and the two men would remain on site until the rescue's conclusion, eighteen days later.

Initially, Unsworth and Lak thought the kids might be lost a relatively short distance into the cave. While forest rangers did not typically venture in too far, the two men had been deep inside, towards the end of the system, many, many times, according to Lak. But it was Unsworth, known to have referred to Tham Luang cave as his 'second home', who was able to deduce where the boys might have found safety— assuming they were still alive. The veteran cave explorer was genuinely surprised at how early, and how fiercely, the waters inside the cave had risen on that June day. It was just a case of wrong place, wrong time, he said—and really bad luck.

In fact, so detailed was Unsworth's knowledge of the cave network that the Wild Boars were eventually found about 200 metres away from where he thought they could be— 'Probably around about the best place they could have been,' he later told CNN.[3]

On Sunday, 24 June, the first full day of rescue operations, a team of about ten local rescuers equipped for diving were on site, as well as about twenty members of the military. The awful conditions would only worsen over the following days as the water levels inside Tham Luang rose. In fact, such were the conditions inside the cave that the local divers could not even get past the T-junction.

'At around 1.5 or 2 kilometres in we saw water. At that time our instincts told us there's something not normal and at the T-junction, the water, it's full. This means thirteen of them were trapped inside of the cave. So after that we walked back to the entrance of the cave and start[ed] planning,' Lak says.

Later that Sunday afternoon, at the first meeting led by Narongsak, Lak was one of several people who told the provincial governor that specialist cave divers were needed for this particular mission. Narongsak was business-like from that first meeting onwards: What equipment do we have at the cave? What manpower? What diving gear? What else do we need? The governor agreed to call in more rescuers, and the first team of twenty Thai Navy SEALs, led by Captain Anan Surawan, was due to arrive at the cave in the early hours of Monday, 25 June.

———

Monday dawned without any sign of the missing Wild Boars. By 5 or 6 am that morning, the Thai Navy SEALs were attempting their first dives into the cave. Rescue workers continued to arrive on site but, if anything, conditions on the ground were worsening.

Cherdchoo Poongpanya is the deputy principal of the Mae Sai Prasitsart school, which Tle, Pong, Dom, Note, Night and Mick attend. The school, home to about 2500 students across all age levels, is about five minutes from the centre of Mae Sai, on the left-hand side of the road as you drive north into the town. It is not a wealthy school but it welcomes students from all over the area, both Thai kids and stateless ones from across the border. Its ageing concrete buildings are painted a faded teal green, and a pair of basketball courts, which double as a school assembly area, are cracked and in need of a good scrub. But the school does offer specialist programs in Chinese and English language; the classrooms are neat, air-conditioned and comfortable; and its teachers carry themselves with pride and a sense of purpose.

Stand in the right spot at the school and you can catch a glimpse of the Doi Nang Non mountain range, home to the Tham Luang cave complex—and to six of the school's students on that Monday morning—just a few kilometres further down the road.

Poongpanya had been informed by Mr Lak on Sunday morning, at 5 am, that some of his students were missing in the cave. By 7 am he was at the entrance to inspect the scene; he was shocked by what he saw. Small teams of rescue workers—including the military, forest rangers and local rescuers—were working to find the boys, but it didn't look promising.

'The conditions were not good,' he recalls. 'There was a lot of water and rain everywhere. I was informed by Mr Lak that they had found rope and footprints that showed they [the Boars] had headed to left side of the cave [towards Pattaya Beach and Nern Nom Sao].'

On the Monday morning, Poongpanya had to tell the school community that some of their classmates were missing. It was a task he had been dreading. Soon after 8 am, as the sun shone down on the students assembled on the school's basketball courts, he stepped up to the microphone with a heavy heart to share the shocking news.

'Six of your classmates are missing,' he told the boys and girls of the Mae Sai Prasitsart school, 'trapped in the Tham Luang cave.' Poongpanya assured them that a rescue effort was underway, then ended on a hopeful note, that the boys would be found alive and well.

After the announcement, no one spoke. While some of the students, friends of the trapped boys, were already aware their friends were missing, the news came as a massive shock to most members of the tight-knit school community.

In the days and weeks ahead, students from the school—some of them close friends of the boys—would begin volunteering a few kilometres down the road at the Pong Pha Sub District Administration Offices, home to the local government, which had become a rallying point for the rescue effort. The school would also organise daily prayer and meditation sessions for the missing team, sessions that were also designed to help the students cope with the fact that their friends were in extreme danger.

———

In a documentary, Captain Surawan would later recall that it took the SEALs about an hour to reach chamber 3 on that first mission.[4] As they pushed on towards the T-junction, they found one section under more than 2 metres of water; the next day some of the higher sections of the cave were flooded to the ceiling. The noise of the water flooding into the cave from multiple directions was deafening. It was a hostile environment in which to operate and, with the waters continuing to rise, it would only become more dangerous.

On the 25th, the SEALs were able to set up in chamber 3 and use it as a forward operating base from which they could launch their rescue mission. But their initial efforts only underscored how difficult it would prove to be. The SEALs were not cave divers, and their training had not prepared them for an operation of this complexity and magnitude.

In those first three days of the rescue mission, Unsworth and Lak were in and out of the cave regularly, on hand as the SEALs made their initial dives, guiding them to chamber 3 and the dive point that had so far stymied rescuers. The SEALs had some early success—on the Monday they managed to get past the T-junction and find the safety rope that coach Ek had used as he tried to find a way out of the cave system. They also discovered hand- and footprints that confirmed the boys had turned left at the T-junction, towards Pattaya Beach and Nern Nom Sao. But they didn't have the necessary diving gear to proceed further than about 200 metres past the T-junction. Another choke point lay in their way, Lak recalls, and in some cases they couldn't even see what lay ahead of them as they attempted time and time again to dive deep in the murky waters of the cave. They needed to work out how they could get further into the cave.

To make matters worse, the water was still rising inside the cave. 'They tried to dive further but the water pushed them back, it was like they were diving backwards and the water was rising up more and more,' Lak says. More SEALs were on their way, but all the manpower in the world was to no avail if the rescuers couldn't get past the T-junction and through those narrow pinch points to find the boys. 'That's when Vern made the decision that we needed three cave-diving specialists from the UK.'

Conditions were even worse on the 26th, with chamber 3 beginning to flood and the SEALs pushed further back. Unsworth was blunt with Narongsak, forcibly making the case for British cave-diving experts to be called out immediately. As he knew, most of the world's top cave divers were British. He also contacted the Minister of Tourism and Sports in Thailand, Weerasak Kowsurat, to make the case for calling the British divers to Thailand.

By this point, the official wheels were already in motion, requesting additional assistance. A US search and rescue team would arrive at the request of the Thai government, which had also asked for survivor detection equipment.[5] Other international teams, such as a contingent of Australian Federal Police divers, a group of Chinese divers and others would follow soon after.

And on Unsworth's recommendation, the Thai government requested the help of three of the world's best cave divers—

John Volanthen, Rick Stanton and Robert Harper. They all answered the call.

———

It was in the 1960s that foreign cavers first began mapping the thousands of karst limestone caves, like Tham Luang, dotted around Thailand. They form when rain- and groundwater eat away at limestone over millennia, forming spectacular moonscapes, chambers, tunnels and caves deep inside mountains. The limestone in the Sleeping Lady is between 200 million and 400 million years old, although the caves themselves are younger; Martin Ellis, a British expert on Thai caves who writes books about Thai caves and runs a website devoted to them, estimates that while the limestone is probably from the Permian age, between 299 and 251 million years ago, the cave system is only a few hundreds of thousands of years old, as there is a single, quite small main passage with no really large chambers or high-level old passages.

Back in 1986 and 1987, a survey of the Tham Luang cave was undertaken by the Association Pyrénéenne de Spéléologie, or French Cave Survey Association, a team of French speleologists.[6] Two teams of four surveyors undertook those first, early surveys to map out the sprawling, twisting 10-kilometre network of tunnels beneath Doi Nang Non. They faithfully marked out the contours and curves of the Tham Luang system, and included the well-known Pattaya Beach. The team also surveyed the nearby Tham Sai Thong cave.

Ellis published an updated map of Tham Luang, based on the 1986 and 1987 surveys, on his website. He says that initial survey was inaccurate, at least in part because of the equipment that was available for use at the time. 'On the landscape scale it looks okay—Monk's Series heads towards Pha Mi [Doi Pha Mee], reached by a right turn at the T-junction the boys didn't take. The main cave follows the spine of the mountain . . .'[7] In his blog post on 30 June 2018—two days before the Wild Boars were found—Ellis stressed that the French map, on its own, could not be used by rescuers who were looking at drilling down from the top of the mountain to create an alternative escape route for the boys: 'It was a magnetic survey with no calibration of the compass or correction for declination. The GPS co-ordinates of the entrance could be out by 10 or 20 metres.'

The survey had been undertaken in the days before GPS became a feature of smartphones. Ellis himself had used a handheld GPS unit—not as precise as a professional differential GPS, but more accurate than a phone (or the French survey). And every metre of progress the rescuers could make was valuable as they tried to find their way through the dark, flooded cave in a race against time to save thirteen young lives. The dive line laid by the rescuers who would swim into the cave, for example, was being measured metre by metre, and each and every metre brought the rescuers a little closer to the Boars—or so they hoped.

It's no surprise that Unsworth and Ellis know each other. Caving isn't about to challenge football as a global participation sport and both men share a particular passion for the caves of Thailand. The knowledge the pair has of the cave was a crucial part of the success of the rescue mission, as was Rob Harper's—the British cave diver would arrive in a matter of days from the UK.

Unsworth had used the maps to extensively explore Tham Luang with his friend, Mr Lak. Between 2013 and 2016, he and Lak—who already knew some of the uncharted areas— explored the caverns and tunnels before helping Ellis in surveying the extensions. Ellis, who has only explored Tham Luang a few times, is not a big fan of it as it is too dark and muddy—'Tham Luang is Vern's passion.'

In 2016, along with Lak, Harper and another caver, Phil Collett, Unsworth helped Ellis plot out far greater detail for Tham Luang Nang Non, the Monk's Series of caves and the main cave extensions. In an age of GPS, smartphones and increasingly sophisticated technological aides, the French map was no match for the updated and detailed surveys that Unsworth and his cohort had undertaken for Ellis over the years of exploring Tham Luang but it did provide the foundation for their own contribution. For example, the T-junction, or Sam Yaek as it is known in Thai, is clearly labelled; boulder choke points are marked; and names such as 'Show Cave', 'Monk's Series' and 'Nang Non Series' provided crucial additional information to the rescue teams.

As the rescue got underway, the Ellis–Unsworth map was found and adopted by Thailand's Department of Mineral Resources. This map, plus Unsworth's presence on site—his knowledge of, and passion for, the cave is well known to locals—gave the rescue teams huge amounts of detailed information about Tham Luang.

One of the trickiest aspects of undertaking the rescue operation inside the cave, even for expert cavers, was calculating distances. Much of the information that was being made public about Tham Luang, and the path ahead facing the divers, had been gleaned from divers and rescue workers who had a less-than-complete picture of the cave. Much of it was incorrect.

Ellis is scathing about the distances that would feature in the majority of maps that began to appear in newspapers and on websites. 'Most press reports have got the distances wrong and confused. My measurements are not estimates, but measured from the survey.'

From the entrance to what became the dive base in chamber 3 was 700 metres. From chamber 3 to the T-junction (Sam Yaek) was another 800 metres. From Sam Yaek to Pattaya Beach (past chamber 8) was 500 metres, and on to Nern Nom Sao, where the boys were trapped, was another 250 metres. Therefore, the distance from the entrance of the cave to the trapped Wild Boars was 2.25 kilometres—less than many of the estimates that were floating around, some of which suggested the boys were as far as 4 kilometres into the cave.

It *is* true the Boars travelled 4 kilometres from the cave entrance to Muang Lab Lae. But in the early stages of the rescue, few would have known that—and the distance from the cave entrance to Nern Nom Sao was indisputably less than that. Ellis says the trip to Muang Lab Lae (which translates to Hidden City in English) from Nern Nom Sao was another 1750 metres—so at one point the boys had travelled 4 kilometres into the system.

Any lingering doubts about the importance of the Unsworth–Ellis map were put to rest by Chaiporn Siripornpibul, a speleologist with Thailand's Mineral Resources Department, who told Thai newspaper *The Nation* that Tham Luang was one of about 4000 Thai cave systems about which little is known; only about 2500 caves across the country have so far been surveyed.[8] Ellis, however, says that Thais use the same phrase—*sam luet*—for a cave that has been explored and a cave that has been mapped, or surveyed, by a caver. His database of Thai caves has 5000 entries, of which 1900 have an associated length—which means someone, at some point, has been inside the cave and recorded at least some basic data. However, there are fewer than 700 caves in Thailand that have been mapped or surveyed by someone who has published in a European language. Without the Unsworth–Ellis map, with all its carefully surveyed detail, the task of searching on the surface for a way to drill down through the mountain—and diverting water away from the caverns of Tham Luang—would have been far more difficult.

Once it was established the boys had turned left, towards Nern Nom Sao, the path was clear. The maps—supported by daily bulletins from the divers and by briefings from on-the-ground experts such as Unsworth and Lak—were like a second meta-guide rope.

In the wake of the near-tragedy of Tham Luang, there were fresh calls for more surveying of Thailand's huge network of caves to take place.

————

At 9.30 pm, British Summer Time, on Tuesday, 26 June, John Volanthen, Rick Stanton and Robert Harper left Heathrow Airport on a flight bound for Bangkok. Once they landed in Bangkok, they would take a second flight to the north of Thailand—along with 250 kilograms of diving equipment—before making the drive up to Mae Sai.

Chris Jewell and Jason Mallinson would bring another 350 kilograms of equipment with them when they later arrived from the UK.

Halfway across the planet, it was 3.30 am on Wednesday morning in Thailand where twelve boys and their coach had been trapped inside the Tham Luang cave complex for more than 80 hours. No one knew if the Wild Boars were alive, and the rain and rising floodwaters were still holding back desperate efforts to find the young soccer team. So while the trio of cavers didn't know if they were flying in for a rescue mission—or to help retrieve thirteen bodies—between the three of them, they had a pretty good idea of the conditions that would confront them in the cave.

Within the small and tight-knit global community of cave explorers and cave divers, Rick Stanton, 56, and John Volanthen, 47, are widely regarded as two of the best cave divers in the world. Stanton, a former firefighter from Coventry, and Volanthen, an IT consultant based in Bristol, have been involved in some of the highest-profile rescues in the world— and they have dealt with their share of tragedies, too.

———

In 2004, as members of the South and Mid Wales Cave Rescue Team, Stanton and Volanthen had helped lead the successful rescue of six British military divers trapped in the Alpazat caves, south-east of Mexico City, for eight days. And in 2010, they flew to the South of France to play a key role in the attempted rescue of their friend and fellow cave diver, Eric Establie, from the Dragonnière Gaud cave. Establie had been trapped by an avalanche of soil and silt a kilometre or more inside the cave and, tragically, after ten days, he was found drowned.[9]

There are many more examples of the pair's heroism— not that either man would embrace that term—and their commitment to their expertise, which has enabled them to save lives in the UK and all over the world. They have set two records—for the deepest dive (76 metres) in a British cave, back in 2004; and for the longest cave penetration dive that saw them travel 8800 metres into the Pozo Azul cave network in Spain, along with Dutch diver René Houben and British cave diver Jason Mallinson in September 2010, in a dive that took about 50 hours.[10] Mallinson would later become an integral part of the rescue effort at Tham Luang cave.

Stanton has even developed two closed circuit rebreather units which, within a closed circuit, remove the carbon dioxide exhaled by a diver and add oxygen, thus extending how far, how deep and how long divers can stay under water.[11]

––––––

Bill Whitehouse, who served as chairman of the British Cave Rescue Council (BCRC) for 35 years before 'stepping down' to become vice-chairman for the last four years, knows both men—but particularly Stanton—well. The BCRC is the umbrella body for fifteen regional UK cave rescue teams that swing into action when a dog falls down a mine shaft, a sheep wanders off, or a novice caver goes missing while exploring a local landmark.

The first of those regional groups, which all function as charities, was established in 1935 in Yorkshire. Over the next three or four decades, more were created to cover the entire country. The cave rescue teams, if you add them up, amount to about 900 people. The total number of members of these regional groupings is also pretty close to 900—they provide their own rescue service, and offer the same service to any other unwitting soul who encounters trouble on a walk through a local cave.

'If something happens to one of us, the rest of us gather round . . . we don't just help our own,' says Whitehouse.

Just a fraction of those 900 people are cave divers, as opposed to cave explorers. ('No one uses "speleologist" because it sounds pretentious and they can't spell it,' Whitehouse jokes.) The BCRC becomes involved when emergency services such as police and ambulance need to be coordinated, or when an international deployment is required, as happened in Thailand.

Whitehouse explains why Volanthen, Stanton and Harper were summoned to Thailand: 'Vern Unsworth blew the whistle and got in touch with Rob Harper in the UK. Rob had only just returned from Thailand, where he had been caving with Vern. Rob went out because he knew the cave, but more in a support role.

'The cave rescue world is a very small one, most people know each other, they know each other's reputations. John and Rick are exceptionally experienced cave divers, they have been involved in rescues and attempted rescues all over the world. There isn't a formal BCRC cave-diving team— but the members on that team are Rick and John, and Jason [Mallinson] and Chris [Jewell, both of whom would arrive shortly after]. And Rick and John would be the first people I would call.'

Cave-diving is nothing like diving in open water. When something goes wrong at sea, the obvious solution is the correct one—head towards the surface. But when something goes wrong inside a cave—for example, a wall collapses, or a passage ahead becomes blocked—your options are not only more limited but also far more dangerous. Before you can even surface, you have to do a U-turn and return the way you came.

Adrenaline is the enemy of the cave diver, and an under-water cave is one of the most unforgiving environments on the planet. One panicked or poor decision by a diver can have terrible consequences, and if a panic attacks occurs, the oxygen in a diver's cylinder can be exhausted more quickly, too.

Although Tham Luang wouldn't require deep diving by the rescue workers, it still presented difficult conditions to work in, with poor visibility, jagged rocks everywhere and multiple dives through sumps that were sometimes very narrow to negotiate.

In other words, it was still dangerous and if something went seriously wrong, the divers could die. It was that simple. So cave divers are, by and large, careful people and tend to take methodical steps to ensure their own safety. Redundancy is a big thing in diving: where possible, divers will take two of everything they can carry—so if the mouthpiece fails, you use a spare, or if a compass or light is lost, you have another one on hand.

Air tanks are often mounted on a diver's side, rather than on their backs, to allow them to squeeze through tight spaces. According to Whitehouse, divers tend to follow a 'rule of thirds' for their air supply—one third of a tank for the swim in, one third for the swim out, and one third in reserve, in case something goes wrong.

And if something does go wrong, the calculus is brutal.

As Volanthen told the UK's *Sunday Times* newspaper in 2013: 'What you want is nice and boring. Underwater, things happen slowly. If a parachute fails on a base jump, you have seconds to contemplate your fate. If something goes wrong 10 kilometres down an underwater tunnel, you usually have until your air runs out to find a solution or make your peace.'[12]

Volanthen, Stanton and Harper—who would help oversee the rescue mission mostly from outside the cave—knew what they were up for when they stepped onto that plane at Heathrow. If anything, Tham Luang was less technically challenging than other dives Stanton and Volanthen had undertaken, if only because fewer deep dives would be required.

They would have to dive through sumps—stretches of submerged passages or tunnels within the cave—that are for the most part not much deeper than 5 metres, which pales in comparison to the more complex 100-metre deep dives, which require decompression stops on the way up, they had undertaken elsewhere.

However, the strong currents on the swims into the cave did make the dive tough, as did the very low levels of visibility in the water—less than a metre at times. Rock formations jutting out from the wall as well as stalactites and stalagmites also contributed significantly to the degree of difficulty.

On site, at the cave, the Brits frequently brushed aside requests to speak to the gathering media, maintaining their single-minded focus on those twelve boys and their coach and the cave that lay ahead of them. As Volanthen told a reporter: 'We've got a job to do.'

That job started on 27 June. Stanton and Volanthen made their first dive in Tham Luang cave that evening, soon after their long flight from the UK. The water was still gathering strength, both in and outside the cave. In a reconnaissance dive that lasted three hours or so, the two men had a chance to evaluate conditions in the cave.

Lak says that on their way back out of the cave after that first, exploratory dive, one of the men yelled, 'We have to get out now!' The rising waters suddenly posed a threat to the rescue teams gathered in the cave.

'This day is what we call "retreat day" because we have to escape out of the cave . . . I still remember every single minute of it. The cave entrance was full of water. Even at the cave entrance, there are many of staff (mostly soldiers) that were taking a rest or sleeping there, we had to wake them up and evacuate from that area immediately.'

Four days into the rescue operation, the dangers of the flooded cave were still being underestimated.

———

Thursday, 28 June, was, if anything, worse. Conditions in the cave were constantly changing, and water continued to pour in the cave, now flooded just 200 metres from the entrance. Tham Luang was no longer accessible without diving. But Stanton and Volanthen still ventured inside. In fact, the duo rescued four Thai men from chamber 3.[13] It would be months before details of this 'secret' rescue would emerge, when Stanton gave a talk to a conference, Hidden Earth, for British cave divers in late September.

At this stage, in those early days of the rescue, Thai authorities had little control over who was in the cave and no one had realised the four Thai water company employees did not evacuate chamber 3 when the waters rose; they had now been trapped for over 24 hours.

Stanton revealed that on 28 June he and Volanthen made their way through three sumps and surfaced in the flooded chamber 3—which would later become the main operations base for the rescue team inside the cave.

When they surfaced, they realised there were already people there. The pair hoped for a moment that they had found the missing Wild Boars, but they soon realised they had instead found four rescue workers.

The Well Water Association's president, Surapin Chai-chompoo, would later tell the Associated Press[14] that he and three of his employees had been working inside the cave for a couple of days to help drain the water when they had decided to take a nap.

They slept on higher ground in the cave but when Surapin woke up the water in the cave had risen, the other rescuers had left, and the quartet was trapped in the cave.

Surapin reassured his men that if the water levels could rise, they could also decrease and would probably do so by morning—but unfortunately the water levels kept rising.

Stanton and Volanthen devised a plan that would make use of the extra equipment they carried with them on dives like this—they were each wearing twin side-mounted air cylinders, as well as two demand valves (a mouthpiece, with hose attached that connects to the cylinder).

So to rescue the men, they made use of the equipment they had and, one by one, using the other's face mask, they relayed the four Thais through the three sumps—which were up to 5 metres deep and perhaps 10 metres long. Once all of them were safely through the first sump, they did it again, until they made it back to the entrance.

The rescue effort still posed considerable risks to the British pair, and to the four men they were rescuing—but Stanton and Volanthen handled it with aplomb. As Stanton said, 'the four, though scared, were very keen to get out!'

Surapin says his team of four owes Stanton and Volanthen their lives. 'If they didn't save me that day, I wouldn't be here today.'

It was a low-key rescue compared to what would happen in the days ahead, but it served to remind those on the ground at Tham Luang just how dangerous their mission was.

It also signalled how important Volanthen and Stanton were to become to the rescue mission.

24–29 JUNE: INSIDE
In the dark

While the rescue operation outside the cave was taking its first, cautious steps towards the trapped boys, the Wild Boars were alone in the dark. On Saturday afternoon they had entered the cave brimming with confidence and full of adrenaline at the prospect of a new adventure into a hidden place most of them had never visited.

Some of the younger boys would later admit they were initially nervous, too, scared about the trek into uncharted territory but spurred on by their team mates, their lust to explore, and the promise of a new adventure. But in the deep dark of Tham Luang cave, the thrill of their expedition was soon replaced by the terrifying realisation that they were trapped, marooned on a sandy slope of Nern Nom Sao chamber, water lapping at their feet. This small sanctuary beneath hundreds of metres of rock was now their prison cell, from which there was no obvious escape.

It was almost always dark inside the cave, too; they did have torches, some of the few useful items they had brought with them, but they were careful to save the batteries and mostly left them switched off.

Although the boys kept track of time via Tee's wristwatch, the difference between day and night began to lose its meaning after a while—especially as they didn't have anything to eat, or much to do. To distract themselves from the growing hunger pains, the Boars busied themselves playing chequers, carefully drawing a board in the sand and using rocks as tokens. They did their best to not think about food, trying to distract themselves from the gnawing sensations in their stomachs, but it was hard.

Sometimes the boys would simply give in and cry.

Tee would later remember that while Titan was the youngest, at just 11 years old, it was 13-year-old Mark—one of the four stateless members trapped in the cave—who cried the most while they were lost. But 13-year-old Mick would attempt to buck up his team mates, telling them not to be discouraged or sad and imploring them to keep fighting—the sadness and the hopelessness would soon pass.

And time and again, Ek would lead the boys in meditation sessions. The former Buddhist monk guided them in the prayers he had spent years learning and reciting after the death of his parents. Fifteen years earlier, at the tender age of only 10, he had watched a fatal illness sweep through his family.

First, his 7-year-old brother had fallen ill and died, then his mother succumbed, and finally his father. Experiences like these fundamentally shape a person's character and help determine the course their life will take. Ek turned to his religion for comfort and guidance, entering a Buddhist seminary in Lamphun Province. Still grieving, the young boy found sanctuary as a novice monk in the monastery and took to his studies with aplomb, achieving Them Ek, the highest level of Dharma education for a Buddhist who is not a monk.

The prayer and meditation sessions with coach Ek were familiar to the boys—whenever they slept the night at his place, for example, they would pray together before bedtime. These sessions had two dividends. First, the meditation helped conserve the boys' energy as each day passed and their hungry bodies fed on the little fat they had left on their frames. Second, it helped keep the group calm and focused, tamping down their feelings of panic and dread as each hour passed with no sign of rescue, or a way out.

Tee was one of the most devoted prayers. His family are followers of the highly respected local monk, Kruba Boonchum, a revered holy man. At the invitation of Ek's grandmother, later in the eighteen-day ordeal, Boonchum would visit the cave to pray with the boys' families at the entrance to the Cave of the Sleeping Lady. He had an unusual connection to the cave, and his visit was rapturously received by locals.

Each night, ever more exhausted, the boys slept near the top of the gentle slope at Nern Nom Sao. The water temperature in the cave, as measured by the divers, hovered between 20 and 23°C, while the air temperature was estimated at around 20°C. The water temperature was higher than it would have been in a cave in Northern Europe or southern Australia, for example, but while it might sound like a pleasant temperature for a short swim or a dip—roughly what you might want the temperature in a swimming pool to be—it was still cause for concern. After hours of exposure to the water the human body begins to lose body heat. Even the divers in their wetsuits lost valuable body heat during the hours they were in the cave. Over time, both the temperature and the dampness in the cave started to gnaw away at the boys, who were clad only in T-shirts and shorts, chilling them to the bone and putting them at risk of hypothermia, which was also a real concern for the rescuers.

Kiang Kamluang, Tee's mother, would later share some of the details of an intimate discussion she had with her son soon after he had been rescued. Kiang says one of his abiding memories of his time in the cave was the bitter cold.

'I talked to Tee about his time in the cave, too, not much though. He said it was dark, and cold inside, as cold as a refrigerator's temperature. He said that he cried once for fear of being stuck in the cave for good. But deep down, he said that he believed there would be someone coming to rescue them. Ek told him to pray and meditate and he did so.'

Outside Tham Luang cave, the rain was still hammering down, hampering the rescue efforts of an ever-expanding team of rescuers, who could not even get 200 metres past the entrance without diving. And the water levels kept on rising.

———

On 28 June, after five days trapped in the cave, the situation seemed hopeless, and the Boars decided it was time to take stock and discuss their options.

The waiting was an agony; their steady diet of only water, which dripped from formations on the cave's roof, meant they were becoming weaker every day; and after five days the cave smelt like a public urinal.

At this point the team had only two choices—to stay put, or strike out and head deeper into the cave.

Ek would later reveal in the first press conference that the team gave after they were released from hospital—although the details were sketchy—that he had actually left their sanctuary at Nern Nom Sao temporarily and pushed deeper into the cave.

The water, however, had risen quickly—Ek's estimate was 3 metres in an hour, which seems unlikely—so he turned back.

In the subsequent discussion led by Ek, the Boars discussed their options. Some of the boys, like Bew and Dom, who had been inside the cave before, argued that they should head deeper into the cave and look for a way out at the other end of the system; a local ranger had told them, on a previous visit to the cave, there was a way out at the other end. This may or may not be true. As Martin Ellis, a member of the surface support team, says, only about 10 kilometres of the Tham Luang cave have been mapped—the full extent of it does not appear on any known maps.

In other words, no one knew.

The boys were about 2.25 kilometres into the cave at this point, and after five days without food a scramble of at least 8 kilometres further into the cave would have posed monumental challenges. Even if there had been no floodwaters or pinch points to contend with, such a journey would be far more arduous than a straight hike above ground; besides, it might also be flooded. And that was just the section of the cave that had been mapped. Who knew how much longer the tunnels would run for? Or even if there *was* an exit, undiscovered, kilometres ahead of them?

Thankfully, other Boars argued against moving on from Nern Nom Sao and trying to find an alternative exit. The team was growing weaker every day, and there was no guarantee that heading deeper into the cave would deliver them from their predicament. In fact, attempting to go deeper into the cave could have become a suicide mission, one that would have made it harder for the boys to be found, while the risk of starvation or drowning would also have increased. At Nern Nom Sao they at least had access to a supply of clear and clean drinking water that even tasted good, like 'normal water', as one of them put it.

In the end, Ek made the decision. He told the group to be quiet, to stop and listen. More water was pouring into the cave, rushing past them, and the level was rising quickly

The team moved up the slope, out of harm's way. The

Boars realised they couldn't head deeper into the cave; it was just too dangerous, with too many unknowns. They would wait for the rescuers they hoped were searching for them.

———

Ek realised he had to give his starving young charges—who were going stir crazy in the dark—something to do. He told his team that, rather than just sit passively on the slope, they should start digging, to try to find another escape route from the cave. The boys leapt at the idea. It gave them something positive to do—which was much better than just sitting around and waiting for help to arrive. So they all moved up to the top of the slope on Nern Nom Sao and started digging and tunnelling. One by one, each boy would attempt to fill his stomach with the water that was dripping from the cave ceiling, then work alone on the hole. Once he became exhausted, the next boy would take over. Eventually, they had succeeded in creating a tunnel 3 to 4 metres long.

Pong would later recall, 'I was confident in the way we were trying to escape.' He spoke for his entire team—the escape attempt, a hopeless endeavour through the thick walls of Tham Luang cave, gave the whole team hope.

In this way, hour followed slow, painful hour in Nern Nom Sao. But the Boars were pursuing two lost causes simultaneously: it was impossible for them to satisfy their growls of hunger, which started in the pits of their stomachs, with just water, day after day; and, similarly, digging their way to freedom was a hopeless exercise—although they didn't know that at the time. But the digging did help pass the time, and give them something else to focus on besides their hunger and their increasingly hopeless situation.

As each day passed, the digging became more exhausting because the boys had no food and less and less energy, from day two or three inside the cave, the boys would later say, they became progressively weaker. And the digging would have used up precious energy that simply wasn't being replenished.

'I think most of us were very weak. We were very weak, we had no strength, no energy,' Tee would later recall after their rescue from the cave.

Nevertheless, the team would not abandon their attempt to dig their way out.

There was also another danger on the horizon, though the boys didn't realise it. Their air supply was slowly, imperceptibly, beginning to deteriorate. Not only was the air in the cave not being replaced but also their exertions used up more oxygen. The level of oxygen in the cave was beginning to fall, while the amount of carbon dioxide was starting to rise. That single factor would eventually threaten their lives.

———

On the evening of 28 June, as rescue workers from all over Thailand and around the world were still flying in, and as the boys were beginning their attempt to dig their way to freedom, a small monk named Kruba Boonchum ˙sangwalo arrived at Tham Luang cave. 'Kru' means teacher in Thai, while 'ba' means respected monk in the regional dialect of northern Thailand. Kruba, therefore, means highly respected monk who teaches, a term that stretches back centuries, to when Buddhist temples were the primary centres of education.

In some parts of northern Thailand, the local people call any highly regarded monk Kruba as a sign of respect—he's usually over the age of 50, ordained at a young age, and has never married; these men don't have an official title or rank, as in the Catholic Church, for example. And while there are many Kruba in the north of Thailand, Laos and Myanmar, few are as famous or well-respected as Kruba Boonchum. In fact, so well known is he that when people simply use the word Kruba in this part of the world, it's understood that, unless stated otherwise, they are referring to Boonchum.

Kruba Boonchum became a novice monk at the age of 11. It is common for Thai boys around this age to be ordained and spend a month or two in a monastery—for example, during the summer holidays—before leaving to continue their schooling. After all, studying the Dharma, the teachings of Buddha, helps kids to become good adults. But 54-year-old Kruba Boonchum, the child of divorced parents in a poor family, loved meditating even before he became a novice.

Over the years, Kruba Boonchum's popularity among Buddhists in Myanmar, Bhutan, northern Thailand, China and Laos has grown to the point where Myanmar's leader, Aung San Suu Kyi, and the King of Bhutan, Jigme Singye Wangchuck, are among his high-profile followers.

Although he was ordained in Chiang Mai, Thailand, and is a frequent visitor to Mae Sai, Kruba lives in Myanmar for most of the year. Each year since 1976, the holy man has travelled to Gad cave in Myanmar, which is located between the cities of Saad and Peng in Shan state, and undertaken 'Pid Waja', which literally means 'close mouth'—for three months he does not speak.

Some of the relatives of the Wild Boars, including Ek's grandmother and Tee's parents, are devout followers of Kruba Boonchum, so his arrival to pray for the boys' safe rescue meant a lot to the families. But his connection to Tham Luang cave runs a lot deeper than that.

In the days after the boys disappeared, people would visit an informal shrine near the entrance of the cave where they would light candles and incense, and pray to a mannequin, dressed in pink—the Jao Mae Nang Non, the guardian spirit of the cave.[1] The idea that dangerous female spirits, or Jao Mae, inhabit caves is common across northern Thailand[2]—as is the idea that praying to these spirits, beseeching them to intercede, can help.

But what of Kruba Boonchum's connection to the Cave of the Sleeping Lady? Some believe the monk is the current reincarnation of the Princess's dead lover and the father of her unborn child. So by visiting the entrance of the cave with the boys' families and praying for their safe return, Kruba Boonchum was actually appealing directly to the woman he once loved.

After his first visit, on 29 June the monk declared: 'Don't
‑ The boys are safe. They will come out in a few days.'[3]

Kruba Boonchum's visit to Tham Luang Nang Non gave people in the district hope at a time when they needed it most. It was huge news, covered by local media and carried live on Facebook. For Buddhists, a revered local monk praying on site for the safe rescue of the boys could only help; the visit delighted Kruba's large band of followers and, for the families of the boys, desperate to cling to any piece of good news, it gave them hope as the search dragged on.

It had been six days since the boys entered the cave and all the searchers had found so far were the boys' shoes, bags and bikes. But all that was about to change.

28 JUNE – 1 JULY: OUTSIDE
International help arrives

While the boys ran down their air supply and used up precious energy clawing at dirt and rock, outside the cave entrance was roaring with human activity. What was for the Thai government already a major military operation was rapidly transforming into an international military effort.

In the early hours of Thursday, 28 June, the first group of what would develop into a 43-person team of US military personnel—including a search and rescue team from the 31st Rescue Squadron and airmen from the 353rd Special Operations Group—were sent from Kadena Air Base in Okinawa to Tham Luang cave. In the days and weeks ahead, this US team would play a key role in advising the Thai government on how to proceed with the rescue, supporting the dive teams and helping prepare chambers 1 to 3 for a prospective rescue attempt. The US Mission Commander,

Major Charles Hodges, and his team were ready; this was just the sort of operation they relished.

Cave rescues are difficult. More often than not they become retrieval operations, with the expert divers heading deep into a forbidding cave, only to pull out the dead bodies of people they often knew as friends within the small international community of cave divers. But no one had ever attempted a rescue like this before—thirteen people, twelve of them under the age of 17, some 2.25 kilometres inside a flooded cave with the wet season bearing down.

The Americans threw themselves into the task but Hodges and his Dive Operations Commander, Master Sergeant Derek Anderson, were naturally intimidated by the challenging task ahead of them. As Anderson would later tell a television reporter: 'The hardest thing is just trying to portray, in words, you know, without physically being in the environment, like what some of these guys were up against, and talking to a lot of the experts, like, that do cave diving as a hobby, were like, "Man, this is one of the five most dangerous caves I've ever been in, in my career," and that was kind of, you know, the hair stands up on the back of your neck.'[1]

At key decision points, when emotions were running high and the pressure was growing on the Thai leaders of the rescue effort to *do something*, to just *act now*, it was men like Hodges and Anderson who would try to remain rational and logical as they made life-or-death decisions.

While water pumps began to arrive on site and search orked overhead, hoisting heavy drills up the mountain and searching through the dense tropical forest for natural chimneys that might lead them to the boys, the most obvious route out—and the most dangerous—was right in front of the rescue teams. The dark, flooded entrance of Tham Luang cave beckoned, threatening death but also promising the possibility of salvation.

But the Americans were not the only international team on site, helping the Thais. On 29 June, six Chinese divers from the Beijing Peaceland Foundation joined the rescue effort. Like the Americans, they brought with them diving equipment as well as an underwater robot and a three-dimensional imaging device. The next day they were joined by a private Chinese group called the Green Boat Emergency team, which specialises in cave and mountain search and rescue, a team of six divers from the Australian Federal Police's Specialist Response Group, and a diver from the Australian Navy.

The Australian government had contacted the Thais and offered to send help—which in this case meant some expert rescue divers. The offer was taken up with alacrity by the Thai government.

Eventually at least twenty nations would contribute manpower and expertise, in the form of either private volunteers or government teams, to the rescue effort. These included search and rescue workers from neighbouring Laos, communications specialists from Israel, engineers from Japan, and drainage specialists from Holland.

It took some time for all these specialist skills to be utilised properly, given the level of disorganisation in the early days of the rescue effort, but over time each team made its own contribution.

Some of the most significant contributions came from volunteer private divers—who came to be nicknamed the Euro divers—such as Finn Mikko Paasi, Belgian Ben Reymenants, Danes Ivan Karadzic and Claus Rasmussen, and Canadian Erik Brown, all of whom spend at least part of the year living and working in Thailand, and most of whom would remain at the cave until the very end. Karadzic, with his laconic style, matter of fact manner and penchant for the occasional cigarette, would become a familiar face around the main operation centre. Unlike most of the divers, he would happily chat to journalists desperate for a skerrick of information and, charmingly, give away nothing of any consequence while still managing to leave his inquisitors feeling wiser.

And then of course there were the Brits. Unsworth, an expert on Tham Luang, had been the first to arrive on 24 June, along with Mr Lak, his friend and fellow spelunker. Three days later, on 27 June, the British Cave Rescue Council had sent out expert cave divers Volanthen and Stanton, with caver Harper to assist. But the British crew didn't stop there—Chris Jewell and Jason Mallinson, world-renowned cave rescue divers in their own right, would arrive on 5 July.

A surface support team that included Martin Ellis, one of the godfathers of Thai cave exploration and mapping; Mike Clayton, who coordinated equipment needs; and Gary Mitchell, who coordinated communications, would join the rescue on 6 July. And two days later, rescue divers Jim Warny,

Connor Roe and Josh Bratchley would arrive. Warny and Roe would be in the water, up at chamber 5, from the day they arrived, and Bratchley would follow them in the next day.

Back in the UK, Bill Whitehouse, the BCRC vice chair, and Emma Porter, the BCRC secretary, also played an invaluable role, sending out people and kit, and fielding a huge number of media inquiries as the story grew bigger and bigger.

Like the Euro divers, the Americans, the Chinese and the Australians, the Brits brought with them hundreds of kilograms of equipment—everything from specialised diving rebreathers and oxygen and air cylinders to side-mounted tanks, wetsuits, helmets, ropes and dive masks. They even brought HeyPhone sets, a relatively obscure radio system used by cave divers in the UK since 2001. Although outdated, the HeyPhone is still used by cavers and even built by the enthusiastic DIYers as it enables communication through thick rock.

In hindsight, it's easy to see that each team and each individual played their part to perfection, carefully maintaining a deferential attitude towards the Thai control of the overall operation while also contributing their unique skills.

When it was all over, more than 10,000 people—including 2000 soldiers and 200 divers—had in some way helped with the rescue.

But on 29 and 30 June, there was still no sign of the boys, and the path into the cave remained flooded.

———

Outside the cave, the rescue teams were exploring every possibility to try to find a way through to the boys. Three main options were on the table—pumping out the water, to make it easier for the divers to get in and search for the boys; scaling Doi Nang Non, with the hope of finding a shaft that might allow a rescue team to be lowered down to the Boars, who could then be winched up; or finding a shaft that would reach part of the way through to the boys, then drilling through the remaining hundreds of metres of rock into the cavern.

On Tuesday, 26 June, the rapidly expanding group of rescuers decided to utilise water pumps. The still-rising waters were making it harder and harder for the divers to reach even as far as chamber 3—by 28 June, the water had flooded to within 200 metres of the entrance of chamber 1—and there was the ever-present threat of more rain.

Thai Navy SEALs Captain, Anan Surawan,[2] who led the initial team of twenty sent to the cave, immediately recognised the dangers facing his men. From the early hours of that Monday morning, when the SEALS first went in and the water levels started to rise, he was concerned his divers were working in unsafe conditions. The water levels were unpredictable, at best, and he made the call: for his men to get further into that cave—let alone successfully rescue the boys— they would have to pump out the water.

So the first pumps arrived on 26 June. Tuesday's task was meant to be getting the pumps into chamber 3—but there was another problem. Some of the equipment was damaged as it was brought into the cave, and would not work, so a call went out for more pumps, and more manpower. And then chamber 3 flooded.

The problems didn't stop there. Both the SEALs and the Brits would need to come up for air as they attempted to dive through the deeper sections of the cave. They also needed dry ground, ideally, so they could check and change over their equipment, such as face masks and air cylinders. But the pumps they had, even if they were undamaged, just weren't powerful enough to expel enough water.

On 30 June, a Thai man named Panom Cheunpiron drove 900 kilometres from the Samut Sakorn Province near Bangkok, where he is based, to deliver three massive water pumps to the Tham Luang cave. 'The government's pumps were too small,' Panom, who owns a water pump supply business called Pop Soop Nam Sing, later recalled.[3]

Hundreds of kilometres away, like so many Thais, Panom had watched the frantic scenes at the cave on television—the devastated parents, the rescuers grappling with nature—and he decided he could do something for those kids trapped in the cave. So Panom loaded his pumps onto a truck, drove north, and installed them on the east side of the mountain. Once these pumps were up and running, they began shooting a million litres of water per hour out of the cave, flooding 2000 square kilometres of rice paddies owned by over a hundred farmers.

But the logistics of laying the pipes even some way into the cave and running them to the outside so they could start emptying the cave of water, were mind-boggling. It was desperate, sodden work, hand over hand, through dirt and mud, in the dark. High-powered electrical cables had to be laid in the driving rain and in sodden passages, and the rescue teams were always desperate for more men inside the cave.

At the same time, a huge team of more than a hundred men—led by the National Parks Department but including SEALs, police and volunteer 'bird's nest collectors' from the distant south of Thailand—began scouring the mountain top for a shaft that could lead down to the boys and their coach. Geologists were also brought in by the Thai government to figure out how water was getting in and out of the cave system. In the days ahead, makeshift plugs would be used to block holes in the roof of the mountain, reducing the flow of water into the cave. Each of these teams would hike more than 15 kilometres a day through the thick Thai forest, in temperatures above 30°C and in high humidity, in their search for shafts and holes.

The US contingent also participated in the search for another way into the cave, as they were keenly aware that the riskiest option of all might be diving and swimming the boys out. At every step the fate of the boys hung heavily on their shoulders. But the exploration of those shafts, each a potential way down into the mountain and through to the Boars, was a dangerous and difficult task. Each narrow shaft—one was as much as 600 metres deep—had to be carefully explored, and one careless or hasty inspection could mean the difference between success and the boys being lost forever.

Tethered to a rope, a volunteer would clamber down—or, in some instances, be lowered down—into a narrow, craggy shaft, seeking a way through to the boys and a path to freedom. One misstep and he could be trapped, or crack his head on a rock, and another rescue mission would be underway. The search teams that trekked over the top of the mountain, both to reach possible chimneys that could lead down to the boys, and to find possible new routes, worked long days that often stretched beyond twelve hours under the hot sun. It was difficult work, with scratches, bruises and bumps a daily occurrence, not to mention sore muscles. At this early stage, the rescuers judged that winching the boys out to freedom through one of these shafts—if one could be found—was preferable to the almost unthinkable—getting the boys out through the flooded cave system.

The bird's nest collectors, from the southern Thai island of Koh Libong in Trang Province, have special talents that were welcomed by the rescue teams climbing over the top of Doi Nang Non. They were another example of the selfless way in which Thais pulled together to help rescue the stranded boys.

For generations, the bird's nest collectors have climbed sheer limestone cliffs in search of edible birds' nests, a delicacy made from solidified bird spit, which they then sell for a handsome profit. Depending on the quality of the nests, which are used in soups and other dishes, they can be sold for between 10,000 and 30,000 baht[4] per kilo—a handsome bounty in a poor part of rural Thailand.[5] Those nests are collected three times a year, in February, April and July–August.[6]

But this mission to Tham Luang had nothing to do with profit; it was entirely altruistic. Like Thais all over the country, the team of eighteen nest collectors had heard about the missing Wild Boars, and quickly realised their climbing skills might help find a way through to them. So after passing the hat around local villages on their island, 2000 kilometres south of Mae Sai, they flew north to offer their help to the teams working on top of the mountain, more than 1000 metres above ground level.

Wearing gloves and working with basic ropes, the team took to the mountain with ease. Guided by the locals, they used their specialist skills to hunt for airshafts, clambering up to points that others couldn't reach. They would work twelve hours a day, find perhaps two or three promising holes that could be explored, and report their findings to the operation centre. There the holes would be logged, marked on a map and assessed as a possibly promising opening to be examined the next day.

At barely 1.5 metres tall, with gnarled hands and feet and a couple of decades of experience as a bird's nest collector, Maann Thonglao is a typical member of the team who had flown to Mae Sai. Why did people like Maann get involved in such an unlikely rescue, so far from home?

'We want to help the kids, we saw the news, they have been trapped for too many days,' he told one reporter.

And while the small team of bird's nest collectors as well as much larger teams of forest park rangers and SEALs combed the roof of the mountain, looking for a way through, drilling machines still seemed like the best option available; surely, somewhere, amid all the cracks and crevices that dotted the top of Doi Nang Non, an opening would be found and a drilling crew could finish the job.

Thai authorities were initially confident that they knew where the boys would be, on higher ground within the cave. Their infrared cameras would guide their drills down through rocky chimneys and lead them to the trapped boys. But dragging those drills up onto the dangerous ridges of the mountain—often by hand, as there are no roads—proved to be a far more difficult task. And the authorities didn't *really* know where the boys were, or at least not yet, so there was a fair bit of guesswork and a dash of bravado attached to this plan. However, money was no object, and in the end more than a hundred holes would be drilled down into the mountain. More than a hundred people were involved in this dangerous and difficult search for a way through to the Boars. All that mattered was rescuing them—just volunteer, put a shoulder to the wheel and have a go.

It was a sentiment that would be repeated over and over again, from the volunteers handing out hot meals to the pump owner driving 900 kilometres to offer some equipment. The fate of the boys, unknown and unknowable for so many days, trapped in the dark, had gripped their nation, and the world. So the teams pushed forward, day after day, despite the tremendous odds, without success.

For all those good intentions, in that first week the reality of the hunt for a shaft through to the boys was just this: The rain was unrelenting. The boys were under more than a kilometre of rock—from the peak of the mountain down to their location in Nern Nom Sao. Finding a shaft that would lead all the way through to them was a dangerous task, dependent on a large element of luck. And all the while, as the search overhead took place, an unspoken reality hovered in the minds of these hard-working rescue workers and their colleagues down at ground level, in and outside the cave: there was no guarantee the boys were even alive. They could all be involved in a tragic recovery operation.

———

John Volanthen and Rick Stanton were frustrated. The con-ditions inside the cave were still dreadful, there was no sign of the boys, and although the rain had begun to ease off on 29 and 30 June, they hadn't been diving for two days. For these two men as well as all the other divers, sitting, waiting and planning while more and more pumps were brought to the site was no substitute for getting back into the dark of Tham Luang.

An attempt had been made by the SEALs on 30 June to get beyond chamber 3—which days earlier had been the main operating base, before the deluge and the floods began in earnest—but it had failed. The British pair had been forced to cool their heels.

That all changed on Sunday, 1 July, when the pair finally got back in the water and started diving. Volanthen and Stanton, two of the world's best cave divers, were in their element, and their progress that day was nothing short of extraordinary. They were path-finding again, helping to lay guide ropes, diving through sumps, battling the currents in filthy floodwater that obscured their vision and hampered their progress. Not content with reaching chamber 3, they powered on. About another 150 metres of dangerously tricky diving and slogging led them to what would become known as chamber 4. A further 150-metre dive led to a canal and chamber 5. From there they advanced a further 300 metres, diving through sumps, wading waist deep through another canal, through chamber 6 and finally to Sam Yaek—the T-junction. The Thai Navy SEALs had been here a week before, as the second day of the rescue operation dawned. but since then the rains and consequent flooding had prevented anyone from returning. To ensure that wouldn't happen again, the British divers were laying cable, carefully attaching it to the walls of the cave, metre after careful metre. They would find a path, come what may—even if it became a retrieval operation rather than a rescue.

It's difficult to overstate just how difficult this dive was for Stanton and Volanthen. Abandoned guide ropes and other debris cluttered their path. Visibility in the water was very low, down to just a few centimetres in places. Over time the soupy, muddy water eventually seeps through your wetsuit and chills you to the bone.

In the cold and dark of a cave, fear and panic are mortal enemies. A lost rope, a dropped torch or mouthpiece, or even a faulty dive watch can waste precious minutes as gear and location are sorted, checked and re-checked. And unlike a deep ocean dive, there is no direct route to the surface—no winking sun, however faint, to serve as a reminder that escape is possible. There is only the darkness, and your dive buddy, somewhere nearby.

Though the global cave-diving community is comparatively small, other divers, including British, Europeans and the Australians Richard Harris and Craig Challen, were capable of undertaking the diving required in Tham Luang.

If they weren't already on site, these men would arrive in the next few days. And of course there were experienced cave divers *not* in Thailand who could have done the job, too.

But the point with Stanton and Volanthen was this: they were two of the best-qualified people in the world to undertake the dives required to find the Boars, and to lead the rescue. And temperamentally, they were up for the challenge—both men are veterans of high-risk rescues, salvage operations and record-breaking dives in some of the most remote caves on the planet.

But that didn't mean this dive was a routine one for the best in the world. They left nothing to chance; didn't believe in luck. Although Volanthen and Stanton had conferred at length with the Thais and people like Unsworth who knew every crevice, passage and cavern in Tham Luang, and had consulted expert maps drawn by people like Ellis, all of this information was in a sense abstract, compiled by cave explorers, not divers. The obstacles confronted by an explorer on foot vary considerably from those encountered by a caver swimming, diving and twisting through the same canals—for example, stalactites that wouldn't bother a hiker much could present a dangerous challenge to a diver.

And then there was the mental game. Every time the pair entered a section of the cave where they could stop, surface and take a breath, would they find thirteen thin, emaciated Boars?

Or when they followed the same tried and true formula: surface, shout, smell. Was this the moment? And if it was, would they be dead or alive?

Failure, once again. The men returned empty-handed on 1 July, but their progress to the T-junction indicated that there might be better diving days ahead. There had to be. The three large pumps brought north by Panom had been operating for about 24 hours now, and while they may not have reduced the water level by much yet, they were playing a part in stabilising the water levels in the cave.

It had been nearly nine days since the Boars had gone missing. They were running out of time.

A sign points the way to Tham Luang cave, deep in the Doi Nang Non mountain range, where the Wild Boars were trapped for eighteen days. (Ye Aung Thu/AFP/Getty)

Their bicycles were found propped against a fence near the entrance to Tham Luang cave. (Pongmanat Tasiri/EPA/AP)

Emergency rescue teams gather in chamber 1 three days after the Wild Boars were reported missing. Soon their numbers would grow into the hundreds. (Lillian Suwanrumpha/AFP/Getty)

A member of the Thai rescue team searches the cave, looking for a route that would bypass the flooded passages. (Thailand National Parks and Wildlife/AP)

Thai authorities stockpile diving cylinders for the searchers. Once they were empty, many of the cylinders were later abandoned in the cave.
(Linh Pham/Getty)

Just some of the pipes used to pump water out of the cave. Here Australian Federal Police divers make their way up the muddy steps to the entrance.
(Cameron Noble/DFAT)

Thai Navy SEALs searching the cave system on 2 July, the day the Boars were found. (Tham Luang Rescue Operation Center / AP)

The news the world had been waiting for. A still image from the video taken by Rick Stanton and John Volanthen on the day they discovered the boys at Nern Nom Sao, deep inside the cave. (Tham Luang Rescue Operation Center / AP)

The news spreads—Thanaporn Promtep, mother of 'Dom', the Wild Boars captain, shares an image of the boys and their coach in the cave.
(Linh Pham/Getty)

Relatives celebrate the news the boys have been found alive and well.
(Sakchai Lalit/AP)

While the world waited for news, Wild Boar fever was evident everywhere. (Lauren DeCicca/Getty)

On the morning of 8 July, a huge scrum of international media waits for rescue mission chief Narongsak to announce that the rescue mission had begun. (Author's photo)

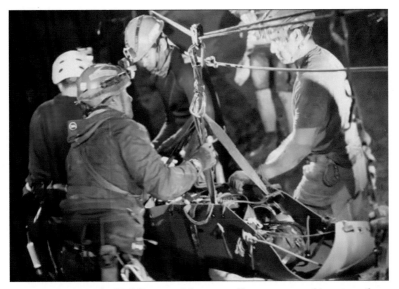

Rescuers operate the highline, an elaborate pulley system used in parts of chambers 2 and 3 to transport the boys in special rescue stretchers, known as Skeds, to the cave entrance. (Thai Navy SEALs/AP)

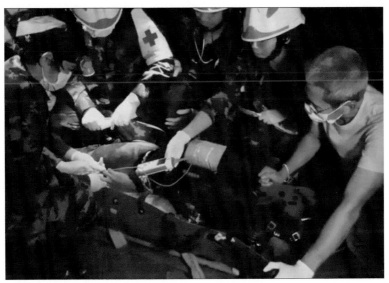

Medics checked the boys several times as they were brought out of the cave. (Thai Navy SEALs/AP)

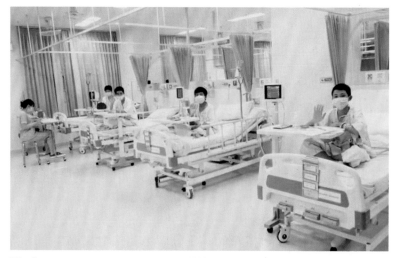

The boys recovering in quarantine at Chiang Rai Hospital, where they would spend about a week undergoing a battery of medical tests, including lung X-rays, to make sure they were healthy. (Chiang Rai Prachanukroh Hospital/AP)

The Boars' first public outing—a press conference—where Ek and the boys were accompanied by two child psychologists. Dr Pak and the three Thai Navy SEALs also attended. (Lillian Suwanrumpha/AFP/Getty)

2-6 JULY: INSIDE
Found

'How many of you?'
 'Thirteen.'
'Thirteen?'
'Ya, thirteen.'
'Brilliant.'
'Ya, ya.'

Volanthen's voice echoed deep inside the cave, his voice, with its British cadences, stretched a bit thin after hours of diving in the thick, murky waters. It was an exchange that rocked the world. After ten days trapped in Tham Luang cave, the Wild Boars had been found at 9.38 pm local time on Monday, 2 July.[1] Narongsak would break the extraordinary news to the world within a couple of hours. Halfway across the world, Brazil was playing Mexico in the round of 16 of the World

Cup—a game the young Wild Boars soccer team may well have been watching if they were not trapped in Tham Luang.

Incredibly, Stanton and Volanthen—who had finally reached Nern Nom Sao, or chamber 9 as it would become known, after hours of diving—had had the presence of mind to film it.

The halting conversation continued, with Adul asking if they will be 'going out today'.

'No, not today . . . There's two of us, you have to dive. We are coming, it's okay. Many people are coming. Many, many people. We are the first. Many people come.'

'What day is it?' one boy asks.

'Monday,' comes the reply from Volanthen.

Stanton, off to the side, can be heard echoing some of his responses in the background: 'You have been here ten days . . . You are very strong, very strong.'

Huddled on the sand, red T-shirts pulled over their knees, the boys continue to speak in faltering English.

'We are hungry.'

'I know, I know, I understand,' Volanthen responds, offering hope that they will be back tomorrow, and that the Thai Navy SEALs will come. They offer more light to the boys, who have been carefully saving the batteries in their torches for days on end.

The Brits have to ask the boys to move back up the sandy bank to make some room for them. The boys, amazed by their foreign visitors who had appeared out of the blackness after so long, had descended the bank towards their would-be rescuers.

And who could blame them? At this point, the vision starts to go awry. Confusion reigns for a moment or two amid a babble of excited voices and hurried translations.

Even as it trails off to the cave walls while the divers grapple with their lights and clamber onto the bank, the sounds of those extraordinary moments echo through Nern Nam Sao— and soon enough, reverberate around the world.

The end comes soon enough. Or the beginning of the end, at least.

'I am very happy.'

'We are happy, too,' the diver replies.

'Thank you so much,' one of the boys manages.

'Okay.'

'So, where you come from?' the divers are asked.

'England, UK.'

'Ohh!' comes a chorused response.

The arrival of Stanton and Volanthen raised the Boars' hopes that their ordeal was about to end the next day. As Adul later put it, 'I only thought, tomorrow I will get out'[2]—but they were in for some bad news.

An hour later, the British pair emerged from the cave and shared their extraordinary news. Word spread rapidly— among the rescue workers, the Thai Navy SEALs, the Thai authorities, and then to the families. It was scarcely believable. The boys had been found, and they were alive.

In the hours ahead the news spread like wildfire through Mae Sai, Chiang Rai and all over Thailand. But it didn't stop there. News wires and press agencies around the world reported the good news: a single sentence on a cable news ticker at first, then BREAKING NEWS, as reports began to filter through.

Foreign correspondents from around the world dropped everything and hopped on the next plane to Thailand. Where was Mae Sai? What was the nearest airport? Just get there. The boys are alive.

———

The moments leading up to the rescue had been entirely unremarkable and offered no hint as to what was about to happen. Stanton and Volanthen had begun their dive late on Monday, 2 July. They would press on, and go further than they had the day before—ducking their heads, squeezing through cracks and crevices, manoeuvring around stalactites. They were path-finding again, patiently laying guide ropes through the caves, through the same sections they had explored on Sunday and then into the unknown. Following the same formula—surfacing, shouting, smelling.

They passed Pattaya Beach, widely speculated to be the place the Boars might have sought refuge, but there was still no sign of the boys.

As Stanton would later recall in an interview,[3] the pair were swimming along with their heads above the surface, talking to each other about the fact that they were about to run out of line. Stanton was sniffing the air, and he smelled the Wild Boars first.

The boys had heard Volanthen and Stanton talking, and had already switched on their torch and started walking down the slope in Nern Nom Sao where they had sought refuge.

'We actually saw their lights, they weren't really in view, then they started coming down the slope one by one . . . I was counting them one at a time until I got to thirteen.'

Volanthen, who was even more reluctant to speak to the press than Stanton—the pair earned their reputation for being prickly customers with the media in the days after the boys were found—recalled the moment in an interview with the BBC: 'We smelled the children before we actually saw them.' After the camera was turned off, the divers got out of the water and spent some time with the boys. Neither man was in a rush to leave again; what the Boars needed more than anything else, after ten days of slowly starving to death in the dark of the cave, was human contact, comfort and hope.

Stanton and Volanthen, perhaps in their gruff way, did their best to boost the Wild Boars' morale. At that point they had no food to share—they hadn't expected to find the Boars that day—but they shared their torches and offered words of comfort.

Later, after the video was turned off, Volanthen promised the boys they would be back. He and Stanton kept that promise, delivering food after more lengthy dives in the following days. Both men knew, though, that the hard work was just beginning. Sure, the team had been found. But having dived though the treacherous, flooded passageways of Tham Luang cave, the British divers knew better than anyone just how hard it would be to get those boys out.

Nature was against them—the rainy season had started, and the dangerous conditions were unlikely to improve. The hard work was only just beginning. And there was every chance of casualties if they had to take the boys and their coach through the flooded passages and caverns. Quietly, both men wondered if all the Boars would survive.

For the boys, the moment Volanthen and Stanton rose out of the water at Nern Nom Sao may well have been difficult to comprehend. After ten days in the darkness, with no sign that they were about to be rescued and no knowledge of the rescue operation already underway outside, it would have come as a colossal shock.

Humans can survive for days and days without food. The body's metabolism slows down as it adjusts, and when its glucose stores are depleted it feeds off glycogen and amino acids. Weight loss really only begins to set in after a few days, as fat stores are eaten away and then, when those stores are gone, muscles start to waste. But water makes it possible to survive for many days, even weeks, without food while the heart rate slows and weakness, abdominal pains and dizziness eventually lead to organ failure and death.

By the time the British divers reached the Wild Boars, the Boars had each lost several kilograms and were well and truly beginning to feel the effects of not having eaten for more than a week. The water they had access to from their perch in Nern Nom Sao had kept them alive, but it had not provided them with the energy their bodies needed. In their weakened state, when they must have been losing hope of ever being rescued, the contact with the outside world and the prospect of being saved would have seemed incredible.

Adul would later recall that, in the moment the divers arrived, he felt as if 'my brain wasn't working very quickly', and that he had struggled to respond in English, let alone follow coach Ek's instructions by translating for the rest of the group. In that moment, '. . . it was very magical, I was very surprised, I was very shocked. When [Volanthen] asked me a question it took me a while to respond. He asked me how I was and I said I was fine.'

Of course, the boys were not fine. Some were beginning to fall ill with lung infections from the cold and damp inside the cave. All of them were ravenous.

But now there was hope of escape. Soon the world would know they were alive. They could abandon their attempts to dig their way to freedom. Many people were coming; John Volanthen and Rick Stanton had told them.

The next morning, Tuesday, 3 July, the Thai Navy SEALs posted the British divers' video to their Facebook page. It rocketed around the world, and just hours later, more than 20 million people had seen it. The Thai cave boys were alive and they would be out soon.

Or would they?

———

The families of the Wild Boars were jubilant. Day after painful day they had kept vigil outside the cave, praying and hoping for the safe return of their boys. As each day passed, the likelihood of finding them alive seemed to fade a little more—but not one of the families gave up hope. Instead, they watched and waited as the hours slowly ticked by. Some had taken leave from their jobs and were unable to sleep, perhaps blaming themselves for somehow failing to stop the boys from venturing into the cave—as if they could have known what the boys had secretly planned.

That the Boars had been found—and found alive, relatively healthy despite all they had been through—was incredible news. The joy of the families—jumping and shouting as the news began to filter out—was repeated in living rooms, coffee shops, street corners and offices all over Thailand as Governor Narongsak Osatanakorn made the announcement. 'At the beginning, we had only hearts and manpower,' Narongsak declared. But now the rescue workers—although exhausted, would have all the equipment they would need.

At Tham Luang, the elated rescue workers worked with a renewed sense of purpose and energy. But that elation was quickly replaced by a single, burning question: how would they get the boys out?

As Adul had said, he and his team mates assumed that, once they had been discovered by the British divers, they would be out the next day. Realisation gradually dawned that it could be quite a while longer before they were out. Time and again, the boys would gee each other up when one was down, urging their mates to fight back tears and feelings of hopelessness and keep going.

They would be rescued. It was just a matter of time.

The three things they had worried about the most, Ek would later recall, were the water, the darkness and their hunger. 'First, the water kept rising. Second, the darkness meant we couldn't find shelter. And then hunger was the major obstacle as it could make us fight with each other.' They had done their best, though, to remain united—a team. And now food was on its way.

But the boys' optimism meant nothing in the face of the weather and the geology of the Doi Nang Non mountain. Mother Nature had other plans.

It quickly became apparent that extracting the Boars from the cave was going to be much, much harder than anyone had previously anticipated. Although the pumps were now working, reducing the water levels somewhat, the cave was still flooded. The three main options for a rescue—swimming and diving the boys out, winching them out, or waiting out the rains and the flooding—would each require patience and time but also present major obstacles with which the rescue teams were only just starting to grapple.

While all the boys could swim, not all of them were strong swimmers, and none of them had experience in diving, let alone the sort of diving this mission would require. Despite all the searching, as yet not a single chimney or shaft had been found that would lead rescuers down to the boys from above. And waiting out the monsoon rains, an ever-present threat in summer, could leave the boys trapped in the cave for four or five months. Thousands of meals would have to be brought in, and there were no toilets, little light and likely not even a comfortable sleeping mat for each of them. And that's before you even begin to consider the clear danger posed by the diminishing oxygen supply, and whether the water could be held back indefinitely. No one knew the maximum level water could reach at Nern Nom Sao.

These were just some of the questions challenging the rescue team as six members of the Thai Navy SEALs, along with a Thai Army doctor, suited up on Tuesday, 3 July, before heading back into the cave. They would bring Ek and the boys basic medicines and food in the form of energy gels—squeezable packets that were easy to transport and that would replace the glycogen and kilojoules they were burning in the cave. After so long without food, the boys' stomachs had to be eased back into the process of eating 'normal' food.

Thai Army doctor Dr Pak Loharnshoon, nicknamed 'Superman', is something of a celebrity in Thailand, with more than 300,000 devoted followers on his personal Facebook page. Assigned to stay in the cave with the boys, come what may, with three of the SEALs, he joined the open-ended mission into the cave. The four men knew what they were getting into, even if they didn't let on to their loved ones.

'They called me, since I trained with the Navy SEALs. On the first day I went in the water level hadn't decreased much, I needed to dive to chamber 3. It was difficult,' Dr Pak recalls. Later, after the mission was concluded, he would reveal that when he told his wife about the assignment he had fudged the details of what lay ahead as he didn't really know how long it would last. 'I didn't think about that but I thought it wouldn't be so long after we found the kids. I thought it would be four to five days.

'I told my wife that I'd go and "see" the kids for about one or two days.'

His wife, a medico widely known as 'Dr First', said she realised after two days that, when her husband hadn't called and she couldn't reach him on the phone, he would probably be gone until the rescue was completed. 'I was not angry. I know him well and I understand that he's [the] kind of guy who wants to do his best. He doesn't think about himself and will go to any length[s] to help other people.

'I just prayed. I couldn't do anything. Staying in front of the cave wouldn't help and I also [had] to take care of our son.'

Their son Power, she said, watched the drama unfolding on television and, though he is young, he understood that his Dad had gone to help some people.

———

The team of seven Thais successfully made their way into the cave, following the guide rope path completed by Volanthen and Stanton on the previous day. But while the British pair had taken five hours to get to Nern Nom Sao and back on the previous day, the Thai team struggled. In fact it's estimated they took more than twice as long as Stanton and Volanthen to reach Nern Nom Sao and the boys, with the last 500 metres—which at times required a lengthy dive through narrow passages—proving particularly treacherous. And to add to their difficulties, each of the SEALs was also lugging four air cylinders.

Pak recalls the treacherous conditions and the flooding throughout much of the cave: 'The stream on the way in was rapid. There were lots of narrow holes [to get through] before we could reach chamber 3. It was [a] different kind of diving [to what I had] practised as it wasn't open water. We couldn't emerge from the surface like diving in the sea.'

By the time they arrived at Nern Nom Sao they were all exhausted.

———

Among the rescue organisers, anxiety about the fate of the men was growing. Dr Pak and the SEALs had been gone for ten hours, and it wasn't clear why the three divers assigned to do the round trip had not returned. Back in chamber 3—now the forward operating base and launching point for divers—communications with the dive team that had advanced all the way to Nern Nam Sao were difficult and unreliable at best. In the end, the trio of divers re-surfaced in chamber 3 more than twenty hours later, and related what had happened.

Exhausted, suffering from cramps and the cold after being submerged for so many hours, the team of seven had decided to stay with the boys on the first night so they could rest and regain their strength. Captain Anan Surawan would later reveal that the SEALs had each used three oxygen cylinders on the way in.[4] Even if all seven members had wanted to return, they simply couldn't—the risk of running out of air was too great. More than a week later, foreign divers would deliver extra air cylinders to Dr Pak and the three SEALs, who had remained with the boys, so they could effectively 'self-rescue' as the operation hurtled towards its conclusion.

If the rescue organisers did not already understand the inherent danger in reaching the boys—and rescuing them—the mission undertaken by Dr Pak and the Thai Navy SEALs had made it plain. It also underscored just how skilful Volanthen and Stanton were at cave-diving, given they had managed to get to Nern Nom Sao and back in just five hours.

Planning the rescue was now underway in earnest but it would not be the last time the organisers would assess the safest way to get the Boars out of the cave. It was far from clear what the path forward would be.

———

Day after day, forest rangers headed into the hills above Tham Luang cave, desperately searching for a tunnel that might lead down to the boys. Now that the Boars had been found at Nern Nom Sao, the shaft hunters were able to narrow down—at least a little—the area they were searching. It remained a thankless, repetitive task, with some teams dedicated to looking for possible new entry points, while others followed up by spending hours and hours in the hot Thai sun carefully lowering a man into a shaft—only to hit a dead end, time after time after time.

The threat of rain still hung over the mountain every day, but largely held off. Every day, at the start of the Boars' second week in the cave, the weather forecast predicted that the heavy monsoon rains were only a day or two away. But, in a major stroke of good luck, the rains held off throughout that second week—allowing the crucial pumping to continue. By Tuesday afternoon, 3 July, more than 120 million litres of water had been removed from the cave. It was progress, but only that—far more water remained inside the cave. But a monsoon downpour could reverse those gains in a matter of hours. Rescuers also targeted the water that had been seeping through the cracks in the ground, from hundreds of metres above the boys, and into the cave. A team of workers was assigned to find and sandbag the larger cracks to stop at least some of that water getting in, and to give the pumps a better chance of emptying the cave.

Although the idea of leaving the boys in the cave—and resupplying them—for months on end was being discussed, doubts about whether it would be possible were already mounting. While the worst of the rainy season in Thailand usually lasts about four months, the rescuers could not rely on Mother Nature to cooperate. Authorities would later suggest that even if they adopted the 'wait-out-the-monsoon' plan, and the rains stopped in October or November, the boys could be stuck in the cave until December or January the following year—an option no one dared contemplate. Meanwhile, however, the SEALs and the international team of divers were proceeding on the basis that a water rescue was the most likely solution. They began ferrying large numbers of air tanks into the cave system, placing them at strategic locations in preparation for a future rescue mission. They also delivered supplies to the boys and their companions in the cave. But there were serious questions being raised by some of the rescuers about whether it was possible to dive the boys out, given their physical state and the challenging and dangerous route out of the cave.

In the days before the rescue mission was launched, Danish diver Ivan Karadzic's assessment of the boys' prospects was characteristically blunt: 'I can't see any alternative [to diving the boys out] . . . the pumping is doing something, the water level is going down, but I have no idea how many millions of litres of water they need to pump out, it is probably astonishing. Diving is possible [for the kids], but it is not safe.'

Tactical response diver Matt Fitzgerald, one of six Australian Federal Police officers deployed to the cave, was even more succinct about the dangers of attempting to dive out the Boars. They saw it as the riskiest option of all.

'It would be terrifying,' he said at the time. 'The cave is quite challenging, there is zero visibility, it's a confined space so it's a challenge.' Even so, on 4 July Deputy Prime Minister Prawit Wongsuwan announced the Boars had commenced swimming and diving lessons.

Outside the cave, there was a growing impatience that the rescue had not already been completed—and a growing number of non-experts proclaiming it would all be over in a day or two. But there would be no quick escape for the Boars. And the very real threat that the boys might die during the rescue effort hung heavy on the shoulders of those, like the divers, who knew best. Some calculated that a success rate of 50 or 60 per cent at most might be all that was achievable.

———

After staying out of the cave on 3 and 4 July, Stanton and Volanthen were back in the water on 5 July and on their way to Nern Nom Sao, fulfilling their promise to return to the boys. Although the 2.25-kilometre journey through the muck and water was slightly more straightforward than three days before, with guide ropes to steer them through subsiding floodwaters, it was by no means easy. It again took them only five hours, and allowed them to gather more information for a subsequent rescue attempt.

In the three days since they had first been found by Volanthen and Stanton, the boys had begun to regain their strength. On the return trip, the British divers brought a duffel bag full of US-provided Meals Ready to Eat (MREs), which were a significant improvement, flavour-wise, over the energy gels—and a hit with the Boars. Their spirits had been buoyed, too, by the presence of Dr Pak and the SEALs, who dedicated themselves to helping the boys regain their strength.

At this point Narongsak Osatanakorn, in his 5 July briefing to the ever-expanding international media contingent, was blunt: 'Now, we worry about the weather the most. In the past few days we worked against time, but now we work against water.'⁵ Once the rescue mission was underway—and whichever method was chosen—the boys who were ready would be brought out.

'It's not important to bring thirteen [out] at the same time,' said the governor. 'They have to train [in underwater diving] for a couple of days, but if you ask if they can dive today, I think they cannot.'

So concerned were the organisers by the looming monsoon rains that they were also calculating how long it would take to clear the rescue teams from the cave if the rains were to hit with full intensity. And there were other setbacks.

Two attempts to install communication cables in the first few days after the boys were found—including a fibre optic cable that can carry both voice and data—in the cave failed, making communication between the operation centre and the forward operating base in chamber 3 more difficult.

But even as Narongsak was declaring the weather the primary concern, Volanthen and Stanton had returned with bad news—the oxygen levels at Nern Nom Sao were approaching only 15 per cent. For human beings to be healthy, the air we breathe must include between about 19.5 and 23 per cent oxygen. Once oxygen levels start to fall, trouble begins even before those levels are reached—your heart rate and breathing accelerates, and your cognitive function and physical coordination both deteriorate. Once the oxygen level slips to below 15 per cent, you can become exhausted doing next to nothing—your judgement becomes impaired, and headaches, dizziness and nausea can set in.

In the confined space of Nern Nom Sao, on the slope where they had taken refuge, the Boars had been breathing the same stale air for nearly two weeks. Various divers, as well as Dr Pak and the three SEALs who had stayed with them since 3 July, had only consumed more oxygen.

And as the rescue operation progressed, a similar problem was developing in chamber 3. Although it was much closer to the cave entrance, not enough fresh air was reaching it through the tight passages, and the dozens of divers and SEALs hiking in and out every day was rapidly making the problem worse. Late on Thursday evening, 5 July, large numbers of oxygen bottles—as opposed to the air bottles, which divers wear on their backs—were delivered to the main base outside the cave and then brought into the cave.

Governor Narongsak then confirmed the cave's air supply was a serious problem for both the rescuers and the Boars, and suggested the rescuers would try to solve the problem: an oxygen line several kilometres long would be run into the cave to try to replenish the cave with oxygen and restore the quality of the air.

Although the oxygen line never made it through to the boys due to the difficult conditions in the cave, it did help replenish the oxygen in chamber 3.

Thai Navy SEAL Commander, Rear Admiral Arpakorn Yuukongkaew, would later relate during a speech at the Tham Luang Incredible Mission exhibition in Bangkok that 'we tried to pump oxygen into Nern Nom Sao. PTTEP [PTT Exploration and Production Public Company Limited] immediately sent us air tubes—like tubes that we use to fill the car tyres. We didn't succeed though.

'It would take us two to three days to reach Nern Nom Sao. However, the effort was somewhat useful as the oxygen concentration also dropped in chamber 3 to 13 per cent. We had a lot of people working there so we filled the oxygen there instead.'[6]

Junk was beginning to pile up in the cave, and the obstacles created by those cables and bottles, like the abandoned communications cables, would add another degree of difficulty for divers as they attempted to thread their way through to the boys on supply runs.

But Arpakorn hammered home the urgency of restoring the oxygen levels in the cave, and getting that oxygen line laid as levels plummeted towards 15 per cent. This, he now said, was the operation's main goal because 'the lack of oxygen in the cave is affecting the kids. At first we thought that we could sustain the kids' lives for a long time where they are now, but now, many things have changed. We have a limited amount of time.'

It was an ominous warning.

On Thursday, as evening approached and the Boars prepared to spend their fourteenth night in Tham Luang cave, four foreign divers and two Thais were preparing for another mission. Their job that evening would be to place air tanks at strategic points within the cave, in the expectation that diving the boys out would become the preferred rescue method. One of the divers was retired Thai Navy SEAL Saman Gunan, a volunteer who had flown up from southern Thailand to join the rescue effort.

No one at Tham Luang cave will ever forget the contribution Saman Gunan made to the rescue effort that night.

———

Outside Tham Luang cave drops of light rain are falling. A pall hangs over the rescue workers' main base. The hustle and bustle of heavy equipment being shifted, the soundtrack of the rescue operation for more than fifteen days, continues in the background. Few people are talking.

At the food stalls, which volunteers have staffed nearly round the clock for more than a week, no one is queuing up. Bowls of Thai noodles, soups and stir-fries sit uneaten.

Dozens of journalists sit on plastic chairs at plastic tables, hunched over their laptops, typing, their feet stuck in thick mud, which is slowly heating up as the midday sun approaches. Occasionally, someone gets up and leaves the area to take a phone call or do another live cross to their home country.

Just minutes earlier, Thai officials had announced the news that everyone had been fearing. In the early hours of Friday, 6 July, Sergeant Saman Gunan, 38, a retired Thai Navy SEAL who had volunteered for the dangerous rescue, had died. Such a death had always been a possibility, given the difficult conditions in the cave but, buoyed by the boys being discovered alive and well but hungry, and by the fact that the monsoon rains had held off, there had been a growing sense of optimism at the operation centre.

But Sergeant Saman Gunan's death brought those hopes crashing back down to earth.

An avid runner and cyclist, Saman had left the SEALs a few years earlier and had been working as a security guard at Bangkok's Suvarnabhumi Airport. On 30 June, the day he had flown out to Tham Luang, Saman had uploaded to social media a one-minute video of himself, wearing wrap-around shades as he stood on the tarmac, about to board a plane. 'Stuff loaded, at Suvarnabhumi and about to fly to Chiang Rai, should arrive at Chiang Rai airport at around 4 pm or so to join the mission at Tham Luang,' he said. He was travelling with medical personnel and more volunteer divers, and was ready to commit himself to the rescue. 'May lady luck stay with us. We'll bring the kids home,' he finished.

'See you in Chiang Rai' had been the message circulated on a group chat among former Thai Navy SEAL officers as the search for the boys had ramped up. Saman hadn't hesitated when the call for help came.

The previous evening, on 5 July, Saman and his dive buddy, another Thai Navy SEAL, had loaded up with air cylinders and headed to strategic supply points in the cave. The two men completed their mission, but when they were swimming back out of the cave, from chamber 4 to chamber 3, one of the most difficult passages, tragedy struck.

Saman's vital signs were fading. After hours of slogging through the cold water, he was in trouble, running out of air, and the cold was beginning to beat him. As Saman fought to stay alive, his dive buddy frantically tried to administer first aid in the water, but it was too late. In those final moments, despite the best efforts of his friend, Saman would have faced unimaginable terror. More than 1000 kilometres from his home, where his beloved wife lay alone in their marital bed, he slipped into unconsciousness in the near dark, engulfed by the cold waters of the Tham Luang cave.

Saman's body was brought to the forward operating base at chamber 3 by the same dive buddy who just moments earlier had tried to revive him. The rescue teams again tried to revive him, but it was futile. His sacrifice cast a long shadow over the rescue workers at Tham Luang cave, and rocked to the core a country that had been avidly following the details of the rescue attempt.

Thai Navy SEALs Captain Anan Surawan later recounted the growing sense of dread in chamber 3 in the early hours of Friday morning when Saman and his companion had not returned from their mission: 'They should not have taken that long . . . we waited until 1.30 am.' It was obvious that something was very wrong.

'When they lifted Sergeant Saman's body out of the water, I didn't want to look because I understood that there had been a loss of life.'

The mood at the base of operations that day was funereal, and the death of the former Thai Navy SEAL sent the rescue workers' morale plummeting to a new low. But ultimately, rather than deter them, Saman's death would drive them to complete the mission and honour his memory. As Rear Admiral Arpakorn Yuukongkaew put it: 'I can guarantee that we will not panic, we will not stop our mission, we will not let the sacrifice of our friend go to waste.'

So in the wake of the tragedy, the rescue workers redoubled their efforts and headed back into the cave, time and time again, to finish the job they had started.

On 14 July, thousands of people turned out for Saman's funeral in his home province of Roi Et in eastern Thailand. The former SEAL was accorded full honours, as ordered by King Maha Vajiralongkorn and, for his sacrifice, he was promoted to Lieutenant Commander and awarded the royal decoration of Knight Grand Cross (first class) in the Most Exalted Order of the White Elephant.

Months later his widow, Waleeporn Gunan, was still grieving the loss of her husband. The pair had planned to have children, but had never quite got around to it as their work shifts clashed and there never seemed to be time. After Saman's death, Waleeporn revealed that she had asked her husband, who had left the SEALs back in 2006, not to risk diving in the cave, given how long it had been since he had been in active service.

'He told me that he was going to deliver stuff himself. I told him: "Can you not go?" I was thinking it was far. Moreover, the operation needed specialists and he was not [one].

'I gave him a Buddha amulet and asked him to promise me he'd keep it with him always. He said okay.'

Once Saman arrived at Tham Luang cave, Waleeporn would recall in an interview with Thai media, he talked about how the kids hadn't been found yet. 'He said he wanted to help people there at the cave. And I told him that he shouldn't dive and I'd like him to stay outside the cave.' But Saman didn't listen to his wife's repeated warnings not to go diving in Tham Luang cave.

Waleeporn recalled vividly the moment she heard the news of his death. It was Friday morning, just after 8 am on 6 July, and a friend who had been following the news called to tell her that someone called Saman had died. Waleeporn began making calls, eventually getting on to a SEAL friend of Saman's. He asked to meet her, then confirmed the worst. She was speechless. 'I lied to myself that this isn't true.'

In the days, weeks and months after her husband's death, Waleeporn would post pictures and memories of her husband to her Instagram account over and over again. 'Missing someone who I will never meet is really suffering,' read one post. 'I want to close my eyes and sleep and when I wake up in the morning I will see you again,' read another. Her grief was consuming her, in full public view.

Waleeporn and Saman used to talk about death. 'I wouldn't be able to live if you died,' she would tell him.

'Everyone must die someday,' he would reply. 'It's how you die that counts.'

6–7 JULY: INSIDE
Messages from the deep

At this point the Wild Boars did not know that Saman Gunan had died. In fact, although they had the company of Dr Pak and the three SEALs, they had very little idea of the scope of the rescue mission.

Outside, SEALs and medics were rehearsing rescue scenarios but, inside, the boys were simply focused on building up their strength and fat stores, unsure of what would happen next. They had stopped trying to dig their way to freedom days before. Meanwhile, Dr Pak and the SEALs concentrated on the team's welfare. The boys were given shiny silver space blankets and plied with energy gels. Dr Pak checked and re-checked them, carefully tending to their minor medical complaints, such as scratches and cuts. He focused on restoring their health and warding off potential lung and other infections after so long in such a dank, foetid atmosphere.

The arrival of the rescue team was also an extraordinary mental relief for the Boars. One of the SEALs had stuffed his wetsuit full of energy gels and space blankets before the swim in and—to the shock of the boys—after handing out what he had brought with him, proceeded to strip off his suit, down to his underpants. He fashioned a small bikini for himself out of some of the space blanket foil, which amused the Boars greatly. As the days in the near dark passed, some patterns developed. The group of seventeen ate together, slept together, shared everything together. To pass the time, the boys played chequers with the SEALs, and hopscotch. Only Titan, the youngest of the boys, refrained from playing chequers because he didn't want to lose; the SEALs, of course, beat everyone.

Pong would later remember feeling great happiness 'because they find activities for us to do and it was very fun, they told us many stories'. Stories, of course, can be told in the dark. Even though they now had food and the company of their would-be rescuers, the deprivations and difficulties continued. The cave remained dark most of the time— they had more torches, and rescue workers could bring in batteries, but both the SEALs and the Boars were careful to preserve the light they had. The only time the torches would be turned on, Pak says, was when the group ate, or played chequers, or when someone had to use the toilet, or was taught to swim or dive. So to tell night from day they had to check a watch, which, after a while, added to the feeling of otherworldliness and disconnection.

The cave also stank constantly of urine. And once the boys started eating regular meals again, the odour only worsened. To manage this problem, they took toilet breaks as far away as possible from where the main group huddled together, digging a hole to take care of business. It helped, but not much.

And although it wasn't quite possible to discern they were living in an environment with a reduced oxygen supply, Pak recalls: 'breathing inside the cave wasn't quite like outside. For me, I didn't feel uncomfortable at all. The kids, I thought they were very strong. Thanks to their regular exercise, they didn't seem to feel anything either.' Pak, whose own child was missing him, would later recall that he would call the boys his 'sons' during their shared time in the cave, and he and the three SEALs concentrated on making the boys feel safe, reassuring them that they would eventually find a way to get them out of the cave.

The hours passed slowly, with no clear indication of when the rescue would happen. No one knew when or how they would get out; it was best not to think about that for too long or too hard, but at least the boys had begun to feel safe again.

But there were also bright spots for the Boars as the SEALs and Pak began to nurse them back to health. After two days or so, they were able to abandon the power gels—not exactly substitutes for hearty meals—and start on Meals Ready to Eat (MREs), which the Americans had brought in by the container-load and the British had delivered. The kids loved the MREs:

eating 'normal' meals such as spaghetti buoyed their spirits and served to remind them of the outside world. In fact, Pak says, all things considered, the boys were in remarkably good shape when he and the SEALs arrived on 3 July. 'They weren't scared at all, especially when we first met. I was surprised. It was a good sign that they talked about what they planned to eat when they went out. They had very good spirits.'

One of the three SEALs also recalls the moment they arrived at Nern Nom Sao: 'When we found the boys I quickly said, "Are you still fighting?" They were quiet. So I asked them again. And they said, "YES!"'

In fact, for eighteen days the boys rarely wavered in their belief that they would get out.

On 4 July, the day before British divers John Volanthen and Rick Stanton would return, a second video was released by the Thai Navy SEALs. It was another rocket from the deep, a sign to all of the families—and indeed all of Thailand—that they should not give up hope. Blinking, squinting, hesitating, smiling, one by one the boys bring their palms together in the traditional Thai greeting, announce their nicknames and seek to reassure their families—and the world. Mick grins at the camera but most of the boys, bone-thin and looking scared, glance nervously at the camera. 'I am healthy,' each boy declares. Dr Pak can be seen applying disinfectant to the legs and feet of several of the boys, grinning as he does so. For the families, and for everyone around the world following the story, the one-minute video offers reason to be hopeful but sheds no light on when they might get out.

As they watch this second video at the operation centre outside the cave, the boys' families are emotional. The mothers are in tears as the footage of their sons, their skin stretched over their bony frames, airs on televisions just metres away from the contingent of voracious international media. Five-year-old Beam, Bew's younger brother, says he just wants his older brother back so they can play video games and football together again.

As various diving teams visit the boys, delivering supplies, the Wild Boars and their coach claim to have heard everything from chickens to helicopters through the thick rock. The claims prompt rescue workers to intensify their efforts in searching for a shaft that might lead to the Wild Boars, but to no avail.

———

On Wednesday, 4 July, two more British cave divers boarded a plane at London's Heathrow Airport. Jason Mallinson and Chris Jewell, two of the British Cave Rescue Council's most experienced rescue divers, were heading to Tham Luang on an overnight flight. The pair brought with them years of diving experience and expertise as well as hundreds of kilograms of equipment that included air cylinders, rebreathers and diving suits.[1] These two veteran divers knew just how risky the rescue operation would be, and that if the 'go' order was given to bring the boys out, there wasn't a high probability of success.

Mallinson and Jewell arrived in Thailand the next day and rapidly made their way to Tham Luang cave. A day later they were diving through to Nern Nom Sao where they met the Boars for the first time, giving the boys wetsuits and other supplies. As water had been continuously pumped out of the cave for days, their progress through the caverns and chambers wasn't as difficult as it had been for other divers at the start of the week. But for the tired, weak and inexperienced Boars, diving out of the cave was still considered too treacherous.

Mallinson vividly recalls the moment he first met the Boars.[2] The boys were in good spirits at this point, despite being marooned in in the cave for more than two weeks, and he and Jewell stayed for a while to talk to them. The desperation of their situation was immediately apparent to him: 'They've nowhere to go but that chamber. They've got to go to [the] toilet there, they've got to eat there, so the smell is quite bad.'

He had also made an impromptu decision to bring along something else—a waterproof writing pad. The messages that would later emerge from the cave naturally delighted the Boars' families, as they were the first communications from the boys in several days.[3] The heartbreaking, handwritten messages of hope were devoured by their anxious relatives and, soon enough, by the world. As you might expect, some of the teenagers' messages were brief and to the point, such as those from 13-year-old Pong and Mark, and 14-year-old Tle. 'I'm safe, don't worry. Love you Mum, Dad and everyone,' wrote Note, in a message that was very similar to that of his three friends. Note had turned 15 the day before they were found.

Others offered more details, and hinted at what the team was going through so deep underground in the darkness of the cave. The youngest boy, 11-year-old Titan, for instance, reassured his parents he was okay and then asked that a close family relative, Yord, 'prepare to bring me fried chicken to eat'. And 14-year-old Bew promised his parents he would be out before long: 'I will help you at the shop soon.'

Night, who had turned 17 on the boys' first night in the cave and who had a cake waiting for him at home, told his parents and brother how much he loved them, while the now 14-year-old Dom reminded his parents they couldn't forget his birthday just because he was away, adding 'it's a little bit cold' in the cave. There was even a request for 'not too much homework, please' after they were rescued.

The longest note came from 13-year-old Mick, who wrote: 'Don't worry. I really miss everyone. Grandpa, uncle, Dad, Mum and [my] brothers. I love you all. I'm very happy here. Seal team is taking care of me very well. Love you all.'

Of course it was pointless for the Boars to tell their families not to worry. But their messages did offer some measure of reassurance, even as the authorities scrambled to work out how they would free the boys from their watery prison.

The hardest note to read was from coach Ek to his grandmother. Orphaned at just 10 years of age, he first addressed his grandmother and aunt: 'I'm fine. Don't worry about me too much. Please take care of your health. Aunt, please tell Grandma to do Nam Phrik Num [a chili paste dip made from young chilies] and crispy pork skin. If I can go out, I'll eat it.' Ek also made it clear that he blamed himself for the team being trapped.

Dear all kids' parents, all of the kids are fine, the rescue team are taking care of the kids very well. And I promise I will take care of the kids as best I can. Thank you for your kind support and I would like to say I'm really sorry to you all.

The responses from the parents, which were delivered to the boys the next day, were just as you'd expect.

'I've been waiting for you in front of the cave. I love you and miss you so much. Be patient. I cheer you up. Be strong,' said a note from Titan's mother.

Mick's grandfather Lek told him to get healthy, and to 'not be afraid of anyone condemning him. Grandfather Lek is never angry at you.'

Night's parents promised he could still have that birthday party he had missed.

Several of the parents stressed to coach Ek that they didn't blame him for the ordeal, and indeed went out of their way to thank him for taking care of their boys so well for so many days. Adul's parents, for example, told the young coach: 'Thank you for taking care of the children and leading the children to safety in the times of staying in the dark.'

Ek's aunt summed it up well: 'No one blames you . . . many people are giving you moral support. Keep fighting. I love you. Bring all the brothers out.'

In the early days after the boys had become trapped in the cave, a Thai official had momentarily left the door open for Ek to be charged if, or when, the Boars were rescued. But that was unlikely to happen, if only because it isn't the Thai way to lay blame during a crisis like this. Rather than focus on blame and culpability, all everyone cared about was getting the team out safe.

The question was, when was that going to happen?

6–7 JULY: OUTSIDE
Mission critical

D-Day was fast approaching; with the growing threat of monsoon rains, there was no avoiding it. So far the rescue teams had been lucky, with the rain holding off despite the forecasts. But that wouldn't last forever.

By Friday, 6 July, it was clear a decision had to be made. The authorities wanted to keep the pumps going as long as possible, expelling millions more litres of water from the cave, but they couldn't keep delaying the rescue. Once the rains started, the gains they had made with the water levels inside the cave would be quickly reversed, so the plan to keep the boys in the cave and wait out the monsoon was jettisoned, at least unofficially. It was increasingly apparent that supplying the Boars with food and other supplies for four months, or longer, was just not feasible. And there was

also the unanswerable question lurking in everyone's mind—
what happened if the rains became so heavy, and the flooding
so great, that they could no longer safely stay at Nern
Nom Sao?

Meanwhile, the forest rangers continued to comb the
roof of the mountain for holes and shafts that might offer an
alternative escape route. But while they had turned up many
leads, so far nothing had panned out.

The weather was beginning to press in, with rain forecast
to resume in the next few days, and the diminishing oxygen
levels and rising carbon dioxide levels in the Nern Nom
Sao chamber would soon force the authorities' hand. But
questions remained over whether the boys could actually
be taught to swim and dive out. It seemed an unlikely
prospect. A search was underway to find full-face masks
that would allow the boys to breathe normally, rather than
only through the mouth; however, finding some that would
fit on the smallest boys was proving quite a challenge. A call
for the right equipment went out to diving specialists all
over the world.

Behind the scenes, Thai authorities were divided about
which rescue plan to pursue.

The military government of Prime Minister Prayut Chan-
o-cha, a former commander-in-chief of the Royal Thai Army,
was watching the rescue operation closely. After coming to
power in May 2014 after one of Thailand's military coups,
then promising elections but failing to implement them,
Prayut and his government were desperate for some good PR.

A successful rescue had the potential to unite a country that had been divided for decades between the political economic elite centred in Bangkok and the rest of the population, who felt they had missed out under successive military governments, or been disadvantaged when populist prime ministers Thaksin Shinawatra and later his sister Yingluck Shinawatra had been overthrown.

Thailand's King, Maha Vajiralongkorn, Rama X, who had succeeded his revered father less than two years previously, was also monitoring the situation closely.

Further complicating the situation, Narongsak Osatanakorn, the governor of Chiang Rai Province and chief of the rescue mission—in fact, the public face of the whole operation due to his no-nonsense daily briefings—had been demoted in April and was due to assume the governorship of the smaller province of Phayao, on the southern border of Chiang Rai. Outside Bangkok, Thai governors such as Narongsak are appointed by the Ministry of the Interior rather than elected by the people. His last day as governor was 6 July but, as he was becoming more and more popular as a direct result of the rescue operation, the authorities agreed to compromise and left him to command the rescue mission at Tham Luang cave, even as his successor took over the top job.

As the death of Sergeant Gunan hung over the camp that Friday, and speculation mounted over what step the authorities would take next, Narongsak's people announced a press conference would be held at 6 pm. This in itself was not unusual; the rescue chief usually held a morning briefing at about 10 am each day and, if there was a major development in the afternoon, he would update the media again at about 6 pm.

So, just before 6 pm on 6 July, the hundreds of journalists gathered at the operation centre outside Tham Luang cave began to position their cameras. But Narongsak didn't appear. The hours ticked by—7 pm, 8 pm, 9 pm. The Thai Interior Minister, Anupong Paochinda, arrived at the base but was driven straight past the assembled journalists to a meeting with Narongsak and the rescue teams. No one knew what was going on in that meeting. Word filtered out several times that Narongsak and Anupong were about to hold a joint press conference, and cameramen and journalists would scramble.

And then, nothing.

Eventually, the same convoy of four-wheel drives that had transported Anupong and his entourage to the cave departed. According to people who knew some of the details, the discussion had been tense, although none of this was apparent at the time. Anupong and Narongsak had apparently had an animated discussion about the particulars of the rescue, with one of the points of contention being the air supply in the cave. The minister had been informed about the deteriorating situation in the cave, but not by Narongsak or the people under his command. That news had filtered up to the highest echelons of Thai society, where it had caused concern, underscoring just how critical it was to launch the rescue.

The rescue chief, for his part, felt that those on the ground knew best. As he would later say, 'Our decisions were based on all data. The operation team made decisions. And of course, the operation management was under pressure.'

When asked about the pressure he was under from the higher levels of government, Narongsak said, 'Our country has many skilful people but we stayed at the cave from the beginning so no one knew [the situation] better than us. The pressure came from various directions. From the national government, each minister has advisors who came up with ideas but those people were not at the forefront of the operation. But I can guarantee that decisions were made by the people at the operation ground only. No one knew better than us.'

The outgoing governor had marked his territory. He would see out the rescue mission, come what may.

On site, both the British-led dive team and the US military contingent were beginning to push hard for the 'go' order to extract the boys by diving and swimming them out.

Just after midnight on Saturday, 7 July, nearly 24 hours after Sergeant Gunan's death and more than six hours later than the proposed briefing time, Narongsak finally addressed the contingent of international media assembled outside the cave. Striking a note of caution, he said the boys were still learning how to dive and swim in the difficult conditions within the cave. They weren't yet ready to begin the mission. However, the 'swim out' option appeared to be the most viable—if not the riskiest—solution.

The authorities were still gauging how effective the pumps were, too. To that end, they had been shut off for twelve minutes on Friday to see what impact they were having. The answer was plenty—in that short period, water levels in the cave had risen by as much as 10 centimetres. And when the pumps were operating, the water levels in the cave did go down, but not as much as they did before.

The effort to block the innumerable cracks and crevices that allowed water to flow down into the cave had been effective, but only up to a point. If light rain fell, the water levels in the cave could be managed but, once the monsoon rains started there would be more flooding and stronger currents. In the meantime, oxygen tanks were being opened in the cave to replenish the diminishing air supply.

On that dark humid night, less than 100 metres from the entrance to the cave, Narongsak summed up the situation. An attempt to extract the boys on either Saturday or Sunday was unlikely if the forecast heavy rain held off: 'We're afraid of the weather and the oxygen in the cave [reducing in quality], but we have to try to set the plan and see which is best.' They'd 'have to figure out a way to bring them out . . . They went in from the front so they have to come out from the front.'

But, he said, a dramatic shift in the weather would force their hand: 'If there's heavy rain we will try to bring them out.' Narongsak's last point was critical. The acting governor was fixing. The weather conditions—and the hesitant disposition of those leading the rescue—were about to change.

———

While the mission to save the Wild Boars was slowly progressing towards the 'go' order, the Australian dive team at Tham Luang was fuming. On 6 July, the day Sergeant Gunan died, an article in the *Australian Financial Review* slated the Australian contingent for their contribution to the rescue effort. Aaron Patrick, a senior writer on the paper, had pointed out that the Australian divers, who comprised six people from the Australian Federal Police Specialist Response Group and one from the Navy, had missed their chance to be 'international heroes' because 'they stopped work at 5 pm on Monday, two days after they left Canberra. A few hours later two amateur but highly experienced underwater rescuers from Wales found the group alive.'

Patrick's article—from the AFP's point of view—didn't fairly explain why the Australians had ceased their diving operations. The AFP dive team specialises in search and rescue operations, the retrieval of bodies and evidence search. Its training focuses on open-water situations in low- or even zero-visibility water and, much like most of the US contingent and the Thai Navy SEALs, the team simply didn't have the right kit for the type of cave-diving that Tham Luang required. Specialist cave divers use side-mounted slimline air tanks, which allow divers to slip through narrow openings. The AFP's much bulkier air tanks had to be worn on their backs, so it was impossible for them to go any further than chamber 3—because of the pinch points that they would confront further into the chamber.[1]

But they were still making a valuable contribution. For close to two weeks, since their arrival on 30 June, the AFP team had helped carry huge amounts of equipment into the cave—including air tanks, industrial pumps and pipes—as well as snack bars and ration packs, bottled water and cooked rice and chicken (tightly wrapped in plastic) for the rescue workers.[3] In doing so, like everybody else in the dive teams, the men had risked electrocution from the live electrical wires powering the pumps in the cave, and had also suffered broken bones, infections and a diminished supply of oxygen in the cave system.

The relationship between the AFP and Australian media organisations had been poor for years. Now, according to the AFP, Patrick's article appeared to confirm everything that was bad about the Australian media.

Previously, the AFP briefings that were available to journalists had been eagerly attended by media from all around the world, and hadn't over-emphasised the Australian contribution to the rescue. Much like the US military personnel, the Australians were careful not to colour outside the lines by offering more information than the Thai military and government officials had released. These AFP briefings were in English, which made them very useful once the media contingent swelled to the point where there were insufficient Thai interpreters and fixers to translate for international journalists. Now, however, they mostly dried up. The AFP's sensitivity over the article demonstrated just how tense things were as the days ticked by and everyone waited for the 'go' order.

Weeks later, a member of the AFP's senior management team would veto their divers participating in any interviews with authors and journalists about the rescue. It was a classic AFP own goal. Instead, they published on the AFP website a little noticed 'insiders' account' of what had gone on inside the cave and so missed an opportunity to share details of their important role with the Australian public.

In the end it didn't matter; the Australian government's official involvement was about to be eclipsed by an anaesthetist from Adelaide and a retired vet from Perth.

———

Maybe Elon Musk was just bored. Of all the sideshows and distractions that occurred while the Wild Boars were trapped in the cave, none was stranger than Musk's offer to help. Like millions of other people, the billionaire jetsetter famous for his big-picture thinking was riveted by the plight of the boys trapped in the cave. But the serial entrepreneur and co-founder of PayPal, Tesla and SpaceX also has a singular talent for self-promotion, plus the ego, financial might and engineering chops to think he might be able to help. So Musk did what any 40-something billionaire inventor would do— he took to Twitter and suggested that one or several of his companies might be able to help rescue the boys from the cave.

'I suspect that the Thai govt has this under control, but I'm happy to help if there is a way to do so,' he wrote on Twitter on 5 July. Urged on by his millions of followers, Musk's tweets kept coming, suggesting his tunnel-boring company might be able to help, or that a pressurised air tube could be used.

On 6 July, while acknowledging there were many complexities to the rescue that needed to be appreciated in person, he said representatives from SpaceX and The Boring Company were heading out to Thailand to see if they could help. A SpaceX employee who happened to be on holiday in Thailand was despatched to Mae Sai.

On 7 July, after receiving 'good feedback from cave experts in Thailand', Musk said he was 'iterating [*sic*] with them on an escape pod design that might be safe enough to try. Also building an inflatable tube with airlocks. Less likely to work, given tricky contours, but great if it does.'

Then, on 8 July, the day the rescue mission began, Musk announced he was in Los Angeles working with a SpaceX team on a mini submarine that would be built in another eight hours, and would then be flown to Thailand. He promised to 'continue testing in LA in case needed later or for somewhere else in future', once again prompting dozens of tweets from adoring fans—and more than a few critical ones from people such as US psychologist John Grohol, who accused him of narcissism and of leveraging the situation for his own self-aggrandisement.

'If I am a narcissist (which might be true), at least I am a useful one,' Musk shot back, and the stream of tweets, including videos of the mini-sub being tested in a pool in LA, continued.

Behind the scenes, Thai authorities had been divided about whether the charismatic entrepreneur actually had anything to offer the rescue effort. Some officials seemed awestruck that he had even noticed Thailand, and encouraged his effort to find a solution for safely rescuing the boys from the cave, thinking it would generate news value—as if there wasn't enough interest already from the world's media. Others, such as rescue mission chief Narongsak, were dismissive: 'Even though their equipment is technologically sophisticated, it doesn't fit with our mission to go in the cave,' he said on the final day of the rescue.

Privately, Narongsak was contemptuous of Musk's impractical proposal for a mini submarine. He had initially approached a friend who worked in one of Musk's companies and suggested they might have the 3D mapping technology that could help chart the cave. But that idea didn't work out. Instead Musk and his team settled on constructing the mini submarine, which would use part of a SpaceX rocket. But it simply wouldn't be able to bend through at least two V-shaped points in the tunnel that ran through the cave. It wasn't even close to being practical.

In any case, the rescue mission would soon be underway.

———

Craig Challen and Richard Harris have been cave-diving mates for years. Challen, a retired vet from Perth, and Harris, an anaesthetist from Adelaide, are members of the Wet Mules, an Australian diving club that takes its cave-diving—but not themselves—very seriously. These two expert cave divers are well known in their tight-knit community, and Harris's specialist skills as an anaesthetist, diving medicine physician and retrieval specialist doctor marked him out as someone uniquely qualified to assist in the rescue.

The pair have travelled the world doing what they loved, deep diving into some of the most difficult and challenging caves in the world, but never letting their egos get the better of them. While the rescue effort in Thailand was hotting up, Harris and Challen were preparing for a cave-diving expedition on the Nullarbor Plain in South Australia. A bit of fun, a couple of mates taking time off to do what they love.

But a day before the pair were due to depart, messages came from the British divers, asking Harris to fly to Tham Luang cave and assist. Naturally, Harris wanted his dive buddy along, so he called Challen. Instead of heading out to a cave on the Nullarbor, the pair flew to Thailand.

Once they arrived on 5 July, Harris was immediately involved in helping devise the rescue strategy for the boys. The British divers wanted to sedate the boys before diving them out; to them it was not negotiable—they wouldn't undertake the rescue otherwise. A terrified boy under-water could panic and drown, taking his would-be rescuer with him.

That's where Harris came in. Was it safe? Would full-face masks, which would allow the boys to breath normally, work? Could they find ones small enough to fit? Back and forth, the discussions between the divers, Harris, and the Thai medicos and authorities continued. In case the worst happened, immunity from prosecution was negotiated and granted to both the Australian and British divers.

———

Before 7 am on 8 July, Thai army officers began putting up roadblocks on the muddy road that led to the base camp and turning back media vehicles. The early risers had managed to reach the area where their laptops, powerboards and plastic tables had been left and a few other journalists managed to slip through. But after nearly two weeks of enjoying a prime position right in the middle of the Tham Luang main rescue operation centre—which had grown and grown as media from around the world arrived—it was time up.

It was amazing it had lasted as long as it had, really, given the tight control the Thai military had maintained on the operation. Look one way, from the media's seats, and you could see relatives (though not the parents, who were more shielded, keeping their daily vigil in another tent). Look the other way and you could see divers in their full kit walking to and from the cave.

The volunteer cooks fed the hungry journalists, who would spend up to eighteen hours a day on site. While one might have expected an entrepreneur or two to set up stalls and start charging exorbitant sums for pot noodles, everything was free—from the coffee to the chicken rice to the clean underpants.

It was remarkable. Later, it would emerge that the King himself had helped meet the needed daily requirements for supplies at the cave, and had done so with a minimum of fuss, away from the spotlight.

The only complaint was the mud, which was thick, ever-present, and superheated your gumboots by around midday each day while you sat at your desk.

But the media's dream run wasn't to last.

Around the camp, orders were bellowed out over loud speakers in Thai and English. All media had to move about 1.5 kilometres down the road to an open-air car park outside the Pong Pha Sub District Administration Offices, seat of the local government. Something was definitely afoot.

Soon after midday, Narongsak Osatanakorn fronted the cameras. Saving the Wild Boars was like winning a war, he said—and that war consisted of three battles: 'Now, we won the first battle, that is the searching for the boys. The second is the most difficult one—to do the rescue. The third one, caring for them at the hospital, is the most easy one.' The conditions for a rescue would be best over the next three to four days, he said, while the water levels in the cave were stable. But they were still racing against time because the monsoon rains were all but certain to finally arrive in the next few days.

No airshaft through to the boys had been found, and the latest estimate from authorities was that if the boys were to be left in the cave, they might be stuck until January, or even February, before they could safely walk out. Oxygen levels in the cave were still running down, too.

All the signs were pointing to one solution only: the boys would have to come out the way they had gone in, through the mouth of Tham Luang, diving and swimming their way to freedom with the help of their rescuers. It was the closest Narongsak had come to confirming what the plan was, and what would happen next—but in typical fashion, he held back from explicitly confirming it. There was still too much to work out—and too much that could go wrong—for the mission chief to speak in absolutes.

The Americans were in no doubt about what needed to happen. All the situational data indicated that diving the boys out was the only viable option. They were sure the plan would work, but they were equally sure that some of the boys would die on their way out of the cave.

The Thai Navy SEALs arranged a meeting with the Interior Minister, Anupong Paochinda. During the meeting the Americans laid it out on the table. Major Charles Hodges, the US Mission Commander, was blunt.[3] Twelve boys and their coach were trapped in Tham Luang cave. The rain was bearing down. If the Thais didn't approve the mission now, the monsoon would decide the Boars' fate. They would be trapped, beyond rescue for months, and possibly condemned to die in the cave. It would be a disaster.

The Americans also recommended that Skeds®, a sort of rescue stretcher, be used to help with the boys being transported in the latter stages of the rescue, after they were out of the water.

As Narongsak spoke to the media that Saturday afternoon, 7 July, Harris and Challen were already on their way into the cave to visit the boys at Nern Nom Sao. Earlier that day, Mallinson and Jewell had talked to the boys about what would happen when the rescue effort got underway. Meanwhile, the Euro divers—Mikko Paasi, Ivan Karadzic, Claus Rasmussen and Erik Brown—and a team of Thai Navy SEALs were busy staging more cylinders deep inside the cave, to be used by the rescue teams.

———

When they met with Harris and Challen, the Boars accepted the rescue plan without argument.

For the two Australians, the actual first dive to Nern Nom Sao had not been too difficult. As Challen would later say, 'cave diving is what we do, so the dive wasn't in and of itself that bad. We can handle ourselves in that environment, that's all right, but I just can't stress how bleak the outlook was for those kids in there.'[4]

That one day of reconnaissance was enough for the pair.

What worried them was having to bring a 'living, breathing little tiny person' out alive. None of the divers had trained for anything like this mission before.

But, the boys were in relatively good spirits, despite the impact the dark and the damp had had on them after fifteen days trapped in the dark, and eager to get out. The food they had been eating had begun to repair the damage done to their slender bodies—some of the smaller boys now weighed as little as 30 kilograms—but they were still cold in the cave.

Harris and Challen had brought with them medical instructions in Thai that explained what was going to happen the next day. And, along with Dr Pak, Harris had also assessed the health of the Boars and whether they were strong enough to be evacuated. Each member of the team would be sedated before they were removed from the cave, so they would not be able to eat anything the night before the rescue operation began.

At that point, the plan was to bring out six boys on the first day of the rescue, so six of the boys fasted on the Saturday night. But it wasn't the weakest boys who would come out first, or the strongest ones, as has been suggested. Instead, Harris and Challen left it up to the boys and coach Ek to decide who would come out first. Remarkably, as the boys would later reveal, they made their decision based on who would face the longest journey home on his bike.

After fifteen days, it's understandable that the Boars had not grasped how big a deal their ordeal had become. After all, they didn't have access to the wall-to-wall coverage playing out in newspapers and on websites and television and radio stations around the world.

But to not have realised, at the very least, that there was a sizeable rescue party waiting for them outside the cave—and that they might need medical attention, if they ever got out safely—showed a charming naivety about the peril of their situation.

That Saturday afternoon, after the media had been moved from the operation centre to the car park down the road, rehearsals began. The hours were ticking down to the 'go' order and, for the divers, nothing could be left to chance.

———

For Ivan Karadzic and Erik Brown, both of whom are based in Thailand for much of the year, the rescue mission would be the culmination of an incredibly tough week. Their involvement in the final rescue mission underscored how they had gone from outsiders to key players in the space of just a week.

Seven days earlier, after flying up from southern Thailand and arriving at the cave, the Euros had initially been regarded with suspicion. No one really knew who they were, or what they could do. As Karadzic tells it, 'It was obvious that we are not super welcome. There is a feeling that this is a military operation and they weren't ready for these unknown civilians. And I can understand this. So for the first two days we just stay there in full equipment and waited. Sometimes we got asked cave-specific questions.'

Eventually, all the Euro divers—Karadzic, Brown, Mikko Paasi and Claus Rasmussen—were integrated into the US command structure. And then things started to happen for them.

'The reason we got activated is, I believe, we stopped being the stupid civilians in the corner, we were part of the US team. Because we had different strengths, we are trained cave divers, that's our strength. The US guys were stronger than us.

'The first walk into the cave was incredibly strenuous, 90 minutes. We carried 20 kilograms and were totally exhausted. But the US guys had no problem lugging 100 kilograms of stuff in, they were like supermen. So they helped us, and we could then help them with cave-specific stuff.'

Brown remembers being on edge for those first two days before he could start diving. 'We hadn't been inside, we were sitting in our wetsuits twelve hours a day, but for those first couple of days that we were there, no one but the Thai Navy SEALs went in. As they narrowed down the plan, they asked if we could go in.

'We got labelled the Euros, even though I'm Canadian.

'So we started working on the cave lines [the guide ropes that would run through to Nern Nom Sao], cleaning them. And we would go in with our two tanks, and carry three more strapped between our legs.'

By Friday, 6 July, the Euro divers were pretty sure they would be called upon to help carry out the rescue.

The rescue rehearsal on Saturday afternoon was time-consuming, but necessary, ironing out many of the small kinks in the rescue plan. It also gave the divers and the Thais, for example, another chance to check and double-check that when someone referred to one of the nine chambers along the escape route, everyone was referring to the same location. There would be little light, and no signposts on the route out of the cave, and even the tiniest mistake could be fatal.

Everyone assembled for that rescue rehearsal in the car park at the Tham Luang Rescue Operation Centre—generals;

admirals; the rescue chief; the SEALs; US, Australian, Chinese and other officials; and, of course, the divers themselves. For 90 minutes they all talked through the rescue, step by step. Plastic bottles were used as stand-in props. Bottles with blue tape on them were used to signify the cylinders containing regular air the divers would use. Green-taped bottles signified oxygen cylinders, which would be used for the Boars. Red-taped bottles were used as stand-in props for the boys themselves.

The entire rescue mission was then role-played, step by step, two or three times, as Karadzic recalls, and several problems with the rescue plan were identified and fixed. This way, everyone would know exactly what everyone had to do and the rescuers could ensure—as much as possible—that the right number of cylinders would be placed in the right spots for both the divers and the boys.

The decision to have the boys breathing from oxygen tanks was another measure designed to head off a potential disaster. Using a higher concentration of oxygen, rather than just regular air in the tanks, would ensure the boys' blood was saturated with oxygen so, if the worst happened and a mask came off, it would give the divers a critical extra five minutes to get their heads above water. It also ensured that, even if the boys were cold and their breathing was weak, they were getting enough oxygen through their systems to keep going and survive.

The divers then travelled to a nearby local school swimming pool and practised, with the help of young volunteers, the process of actually diving and rescuing children in the water of the cave. These sessions were crucial to the last-minute fine tuning of the rescue plan. Calls had already gone out to the international diving community to find small wetsuits and full-face masks for the boys to wear on their way out, and this equipment was tested at the pool. Even though it had been decided which divers would bring the boys out and who would be positioned at key points along the exit route, all the divers were involved in the practice sessions. For example, some members of the rescue team, such as Karadzic, weren't familiar with the full-face masks the boys would use; the straps had to be pulled tight to ensure they would fit over the faces of the smallest boys.

Meanwhile, the back and forth continued over when to give the go-ahead order. Narongsak had asked the divers to devise and propose a plan. The Americans had made their case and were certain it was time. The British divers, who would lead the rescue mission, were ready to go, as were the Thai Navy SEALs and the support teams, including the Australians, the Chinese and various other nationalities.

As the public face of the rescue, Narongsak was popular with the local people but he still faced internal challenges and was, to some extent, politically weak. The Thai Army and Navy were heavily involved in the rescue, the national government was monitoring developments closely and the King himself had taken a close interest in the situation: each day, staff from the royal household visited the cave to find out what the rescue teams needed, and the subsequent deliveries would take place away from the cameras.

The commander of the Thai Navy SEALs, Rear Admiral Arpakorn Yuukongkaew,[5] who had authority over all the divers on site, had also urged the divers to formulate a rescue plan, as he would later recall: 'I talked to diver team and told them to come up with a plan and I'd propose it to "the top". This was crucial because I told them: "If we don't do anything, we have nothing in return."

'We couldn't wait too long. If the oxygen dropped to 12 per cent the kids' condition would be worse. Moreover, the cave would be full of water. We thought if we began the operation and it was 50 per cent successful, it was still better than nothing.'

But for all the involvement of the national government, the military and the royal household, Narongsak was under no illusions about what could happen—both to the Boars, and to him personally. 'The worst-case scenario was included in our plans but we believed in our well-thought and well-planned mission. We were also lucky that our rescue operation was successful, otherwise my situation would be so different.

'Whatever happened, it would be me to take full responsibility as I was in charge of the operation. There was no way to avoid the responsibility.'

The weather forecast indicated they had a three- or four-day window for the rescue. The divers were primed and ready to go. They had rehearsed and finessed the plan as much as they could.

Narongsak may have formally given the order to begin the rescue, but in reality that assent had to be given by the higher echelons of Thai society. The government of Thai Prime Minister Prayut Chan-o-cha had approved it. The King fully supported the rescue operation. It was time.

But if it all went wrong, the chief of the rescue mission would carry the can.

8 JULY: INSIDE
Sunday, 10.08 am

Sunday, 8 July, began like any other morning in Tham Luang cave. The Wild Boars woke early, as they always did, in the dark. The air inside the cave was humid, but as they entered their sixteenth day perched on Nern Nom Sao, the boys were still feeling the cold despite the space blankets and extra clothes they had been given.

After being trapped for so long, the sandy bank on which they were perched felt smaller than ever. Of course, it was still only 5 to 6 metres wide, and about 20–25 metres deep, from the water's edge to the back of the cave, while the slope, at various points, was as steep as 30 degrees. They must have felt as if the walls were closing in on them. The novelty of energy gels and Meals Ready to Eat had worn off, and the conditions in the cave—the darkness, the smell and the constant chill— were wearing them down.

The day before, some of the British divers as well as Richard Harris, the Australian doctor, had visited and given them a detailed account of the rescue plan, which of course had been accepted by the Boars' families, despite their fears that it could end in disaster and tragedy.

The boys were desperate to see their families again, to go home, sleep in their own beds. They were ready to be kids again, to stop being brave, to breathe fresh air, ride around on their bikes, play football and see their friends at school. The day had dawned with the promise of all these things and more. It was time.

After fasting in preparation for the rescue, six of the boys had woken up hungry. But the rescue divers faced dawn that morning with a faint feeling of dread. Men like Rick Stanton and John Volanthen, Chris Jewell and Jason Mallinson, Richard Harris and Craig Challen, had all been in this situation before. They'd participated in some of the riskiest, most extreme cave rescues the world had ever seen. They'd lost friends and undertaken salvage operations; they'd helped bring back the bodies of the dead. Maybe even cried afterwards, when it was all done. They'd also saved lives, brought people back to the surface—people who'd had no hope of being rescued. These guys were the best of the best.

The diving itself may not have been the most technically difficult, the most arduous, or the deepest they had ever experienced. But nothing like this had ever been attempted before; usually, by the time help arrives, it is already too late. There was no base line against which to measure themselves.

And no one in the rescue team had ever undertaken a mission like this before, with many millions of people watching, hoping, praying they would succeed.

But other divers in the rescue team had far less experience, even none at all, in undertaking a high-risk rescue with such a precious, vulnerable cargo.

The mission had been approved by the Thai King and the government, and reviewed by teams of experts. In theory at least, it had a good chance of succeeding. But there were so many factors that could go wrong at any point; they couldn't anticipate everything. And the worst-case scenario—that some or even all of the boys would lose their lives—had been war-gamed again and again. If one of the boys woke up, panicked and ripped off his mask in an underwater section of the cave, he could endanger the life of his rescuer, as well as himself.

Everything possible had been done to prepare for the rescue mission. For the boys, there were special wetsuits that would ensure they didn't lose too much body heat on the journey out as well as full-face masks to fit the smallest of them. The oxygen and air cylinders had been placed at strategic points in various chambers throughout the cave.

But for all their careful preparations, most of the rescuers expected multiple casualties. Rear Admiral Arpakorn Yuukongkaew expected some of the boys would die on the way out while Major Charles Hodges put a figure on it, assessing that only eight to ten Boars would survive the rescue. Mallinson was confident he would be able to play his part and help get the boys out, but he 'was not fully confident of getting them out alive'. And as Challen would later recall, 'it wasn't dangerous for us but I can't emphasise enough how dangerous it was for the kids. It was absolutely life and death. We didn't expect to be getting thirteen people out of there alive.'[1]

Richard Harris was perhaps the most pessimistic of all. He would tell a conference in Melbourne, Australia, in late September, 'Personally, I honestly thought there was zero chance of success. I honestly thought there was no chance of it working. We set up a system for some feedback to come back after the first one or two kids [began their dive out] to me. If they hadn't survived the first sump, which was the longest one but not the most difficult one, I was going to say that's all I can do and walk away at that point.'

Still, no official estimate had been made of how many of the boys would survive the rescue attempt. How could such a thing be calculated? It was time to go.

———

In the days before the rescue mission began, work was done behind the scenes by men like Josh Morris and Thanet Natisri to get the 'dive them out' option over the line with the Thais running the mission.

The pair acted as emissaries between the foreigners and the Thais, sharing key pieces of information at opportune moments between the divers and high-ranking Thai military officials—some of whom were unaware, on 5 July, just how bad the air supply had become.

It was the deteriorating air conditions that was one of the key reasons the rescue went ahead when it did.

After final meetings were held outside the cave, with Thai officials checking every last detail of the plan, the rescue mission finally began at 10.08 am on Sunday, 8 July, when a team of thirteen international divers entered Tham Luang cave. Heavy rain had fallen overnight and, later that day, it would fall again, but at this hour the skies over Mae Sai were grey and threatening rain, underlining the urgency of the rescue mission.

The thirteen divers—Rick Stanton, John Volanthen, Chris Jewell, Jason Mallinson, Richard Harris, Craig Challen, Claus Rasmussen, Mikko Paasi, Erik Brown, Ivan Karadzic, Jim Warny, Josh Bratchley and Connor Roe—are some of the best cave divers in the world. They were closely supported by five Thai Navy SEALs as well as dozens of personnel from the Thai military, the United States, China and Australia who were positioned in the first three chambers of the cave. Lights, dozens of air tanks and radios that could communicate with the outside world had been set up in chamber 3—as had makeshift medical facilities, so the boys could be checked on as they came out.

Outside the cave, the area around the entrance swarmed with members of the Thai military, rescuers and medics. Thirteen ambulances were on standby, as they had been for days, while helicopters were prepped and ready to ferry the boys 70 kilometres to Chiang Rai Prachanukroh Hospital, where medical staff waited to receive them.

The eyes of the entire world were on this remote corner of northern Thailand.

———

About two hours after the rescue mission began, Narongsak Osatanakorn fronted the ever-expanding contingent of international media. The huge mountain range of Doi Nang Non, shrouded in clouds and mist, loomed over the new make-shift media centre and served as a constant reminder that the boys' fate was about to be decided.

The new media centre was in a concrete car park, with tarpaulins and electrical cables strung overhead and the same fold-out plastic tables and wobbly chairs. Internet access was patchy at times, as hundreds of journalists used their phones as hotspots and crowded the 4G network to send vision back to offices around the world.

Narongsak began his press conference with words that would reverberate around the world: 'Today we are most ready, today is D-Day. At 10 am today thirteen foreign divers went in to extract the children along with five Thai Navy SEALs.'

The volunteers, some of whom had decamped with the media to the new location to keep cooking and handing out free meals, fell silent. Some gasped and cheered as Narongsak continued to speak. A hushed excitement fell over the crowd gathered outside the operations centre as Narongsak continued: 'We can say they are all international all-stars involved in this diving operation and we selected five of our best who can work with them.

'The kids are very determined and they are in high spirits. All thirteen kids have been informed about the operation and they are ready to come out.

'If we don't start now, we might lose the chance.'

At this stage, although the water levels in the cave had receded by as much as 30 centimetres in some sections of the cave, the divers had, at most, a three-day window before the forecast rain would make a rescue impossible. Narongsak estimated that the first of the Boars would not emerge from the cave until at least 9 pm that evening—eleven hours after the rescue began—and warned that the mission would not be finished in just one day: 'It will take time. It's not that we start 10 am today and everything is done. We will continue the mission until the last one is out.'

———

Inside the cave, the thirteen rescue divers had begun their slow journey through the nine chambers from the entrance to Nern Nom Sao. They were all aware of the incredible responsibility hanging heavily on their shoulders; it didn't need to be acknowledged aloud. Most of the men would position themselves at strategic points along the route, while Harris and four British divers—Volanthen, Stanton, Jewell and Mallinson—would travel all the way to the boys, where the Brits would be in charge.

Contrary to reports at the time, the boys were not assigned two divers each. That wasn't logistically possible, given how narrow and difficult some sections of the cave were. But, almost every step of the way, a second diver would assist the man bringing them out. Each of the four British divers would take one boy all the way from chamber 9 to the entrance.

The Brits as well as Harris and his dive buddy Challen went in first, as they had the longest dive ahead of them. Travelling in pairs, the six men set out from chamber 3, where the diving began in earnest, at about twenty-minute intervals. Over the next few hours they slowly made their way to predetermined points along the route. In spite of the lower water levels, the conditions were still very tough.

Challen, Rasmussen and Paasi were stationed in chamber 8, the first stop on the return journey for the four Brits as each came through with one boy. The route from chamber 9, Nern Nom Sao, to chamber 8 included a 350-metre dive that would be one of the hardest sections to negotiate. Volanthen, Stanton, Jewell and Mallinson could walk part of the 150-metre section between chamber 8 and chamber 7, but they would also have to negotiate a canal. This section was tough because the water levels there had dropped to the point where they would have to carry the boys while negotiating thick mud and rocky obstacles; the extra pairs of hands to assist in that section would prove invaluable.

The journey from chamber 7 to chamber 6 required another 300-metre dive for the Brits and the Boars, and passage through what was arguably the most difficult point— Sam Yaek, the T-junction. At this point, the tunnel narrows considerably, creating one of the tightest pinch points, and the four rescuers would also have to scramble up and down some rocks while keeping the boys safe, and moving. All the way along, stalactites and stalagmites, sometimes underwater and sometimes exposed, always offered potential obstacles that could endanger both the divers and the boys. And in the submerged sections, the muddy water reduced visibility to almost nothing, making diving that much harder.

The rescue plan called for Challen, a retired vet, to be ready to deliver a 'top up' injection to the boys in chamber 8 to keep the boys sedated, if necessary. Harris revealed at a conference in late September that the night before the first rescue mission, he held a practice session for the divers involving a plastic drink bottle so they could get an (improvised) feel for what delivering an injection was like.[2]

The British rescuers were prepped and ready to deliver top-up injections on the way out, too, and the instruction from Harris was to err on the side of keeping the boys sedated.

In chamber 6, Karadzic and Brown would be ready with air and oxygen tanks, and more medicine to inject into the boys if the effects of the sedative were starting to wear off.

Between chambers 6 and 5, there was another 150-metre dive, then a 150-metre canal. And in chamber 5, Roe and Warny would be waiting with more air, oxygen and medicine to help the divers and each of the boys through to chamber 3. Along the way, there were two more dives of about 150 metres each to make before, finally, they reached chamber 3.

Chamber 3 was relatively huge—perhaps half the size of a school gymnasium, according to Brown, and big enough that you could project a movie onto one of its walls—and teeming with people. In all, there were perhaps another 150 rescuers stationed between chamber 3 and the exit.

In chamber 3 each boy's vital signs would be checked by doctors and gauze placed over his eyes to protect them from the light outside the cave. Then he would be placed in a Sked stretcher and loaded onto the elaborate pulley system, or highline, which made it simpler and quicker to transport each boy through to the entrance. But some sections simply couldn't accommodate the highline, so he would still have to pass through a couple of hundred hands as he was brought out of the cave.

In theory, it sounded straightforward. The planning had been methodical, the staging of equipment and men meticulous. The mission was high risk, but it *could* work. But no one could anticipate, or plan for, how the boys would handle the situation. All the preparation and medication in the world would count for nought if one of the boys woke up mid-dive and panicked. If that happened, Thai authorities would be counting the number of casualties, not lives saved.

All of this and more—perhaps even what it would feel like if they succeeded—ran through the thirteen divers' minds as they took up their positions in the Tham Luang cave.

Meanwhile, at Nern Nom Sao, the boys were nervous; they knew what, and who, was coming. Although six of the Boars had fasted the night before, it was decided at some point that the divers would attempt to bring out only four boys that Sunday. After talking it through with coach Ek and the Thai Navy SEALs, who had stayed with them since they were found, they'd decided among themselves who would go out first.

Volanthen, Stanton, Jewell, Mallinson and Harris had arrived at Nern Nom Sao after swimming and diving for close to two hours. Now it was time to get started.

———

Richard 'Harry' Harris was ready to prime the needle; it was time to sedate the first Wild Boar. In consultation with Dr Pak as well as a team of Thai doctors outside the cave, Harris had calculated approximately what dose each boy would need. He would give each of the boys Alprazolam—more commonly known as Xanax, an anti-anxiety drug—by mouth, then inject him in each leg with Ketamine, a sedative.[3]

Harris had devised a plan for handling the injections. Although he had visited them the day before, and someone had read the boys instructions in Thai, telling them what would happen at the start of the rescue, he didn't want the Boars watching while one of their mates was injected and then submerged. So he asked the Navy SEALs to take the other Boars up to the top of the slope in Nern Nom Sao.

The instructions were to the point. First, each of the boys to be taken out that day would swallow a tablet, which would make him feel a bit strange, and then he would join Harris at the bottom of the bank, near the water. There, he would be injected in the legs and go to sleep. When he woke up again, he would be in a hospital bed, out of the cave. The boys had listened intently to this plan and nodded along, questioning

149

nothing. As the rescuers went about prepping the four boys one by one in their deliberate, careful fashion, they made the most of the boys' relative ignorance of what lay ahead, using it to their advantage.

While Harris prepared his sedatives, Dr Pak briefed the kids again about the rescue plan. As he spoke to the boys in Thai, the brave doctor, who had already spent seven nights in the cave with the three SEALs, paid careful attention to whether or not the first four boys were ready for the mission.

They were; they were eager to get started. Down by the water line, under unsteady torchlights, Richard Harris was ready. He plunged the needle into Note's leg; he would be the first boy out.

'They seemed to be very confident and having Dr Harris helped a great deal. He was in charge of giving the kids "medicine" and he was great,' Pak says. 'He had techniques to talk to the kids, he hugged them and he was so great with them. Dr Harris was like a father or grandfather figure to them.'

Harris's calm, reassuring bedside manner was vital in getting the kids to the point where they were ready to dive, and he left nothing to chance. Once the first boy was sedated, and his full-face mask fitted, Harris took the boy down to the water and pushed his head under water. It may have seemed like the wrong thing to do, but it was absolutely critical to test each full-face mask to make sure it fitted properly. After all, better to discover a problem immediately rather than half a kilometre into the rescue mission.

After about 30 seconds, which passed with agonising slowness, the first Boar started breathing again; the mask worked, and the sedative had been administered in the right dose. Over the next three days, Harris would repeat this breathing test twelve times. The plan was to keep the boys completely 'under' at least as far as chamber 3. By the end, Harris had taken to horrifying the Brits with the procedure: 'Watch this, he will stop breathing for a second . . .'

Narongsak would later confirm that the sedation of the boys was supposed to be kept quiet, but Prime Minister Prayut Chan-o-cha let it slip.

After so long in the cave, a couple of the boys showed signs of the early stages of pneumonia; it was remarkable that more of them weren't ill. But the last boy to leave on that first day gave Harris a scare. After the doctor administered the injections in each leg, the boy 'behaved like a bad kid with a chest infection under anaesthetic—breath holding, he was over-sedated', he later recalled at a medical conference in Sydney, Australia. He laid down on the sand with the boy for half an hour, spooning him and listening to his breathing to ensure that his airways remained open. It was one of many tense moments over the next three days. He later said he was 'thinking this is what I predicted would happen, this is going to go really badly. Then he sort of fired up. He ended up needing another dose to put him back [under] in the water about 200 metres down the track.'

To minimise the risk to the rescuers on the way out, it had been decided to err on the side of caution and administer two to four top-ups to each boy as he was brought out of the cave.

Harris had consulted Thai medics and Australian ones about how to handle the situation, but he was the doctor on site, so he ultimately had to make the call.

For the Brits, the sedatives had been non-negotiable. They simply wouldn't have undertaken the mission without Harris, in the cave, administering the doses that put the boys under.

———

Although the divers knew what to expect, and the water temperature was holding up well, still hovering around 20°C, those first few moments in the water were still a shock. It was simply the enormity of what they were about to do. Each man had the life of a young boy in his hands; each of the boys was, at best, semiconscious and, even if he had been fully conscious, he would have been unable to fend for himself in this incredibly dangerous place.

It is unclear whether all the boys were completely unconscious. Some of the rescuers, such as Rick Stanton, have insisted they were, and would remember nothing. Ivan Karadzic, however, recalls that at least one of the boys had his eyes open, and was speaking Thai—'though my Thai isn't good enough to know what he was saying'—as they came out of the cave. Though he agrees with Stanton that it's unlikely the boys remember much, if anything, about the rescue mission.

Once Mallinson was in the water with Note, the pair submerged for the first 350-metre dive, which took them past

Pattaya Beach to chamber 8. As well as the wetsuit and full-face mask, Note was wearing both a buoyancy device and a harness that would keep him attached to Mallinson and also give the diver a handle to grab onto. Note also had an oxygen cylinder strapped to his front, and was positioned beneath Mallinson to ensure he didn't hit his head on the roof of the cave. Mallinson wasn't concerned about his own safety, but he was nervous about the fate of the 15-year-old he held in his hands. He, and the divers who would come after him, were in completely uncharted territory.

'I was very nervous when we took them from the end point and you got into that first flooded section,' Mallinson says. 'Until you got a feel for the way their breathing rhythm was going, it was very nervous for the first five or ten minutes, you just wanted to see those air bubbles coming out of that mask all the time.'

It was dark in the water, but the lights each diver wore helped him to see. The next step was to locate the path-finding line, which would help him to pull them through. Sometimes, the boy would be positioned to the left or the right of the diver, depending on where the guideline had been laid. At other times, as they made their way out of Tham Luang cave, the diver was so close to the boy that he could feel and see the air bubbles that would slowly escape from the face mask his young charge wore.

To get through the narrowest choke points, the diver would push the boy through first with the help of the other divers stationed throughout the cave. It was a painfully slow process, and took much longer than the couple of hours it had taken for them to reach Nern Nom Sao.

While the divers did their best, it was sometimes impossible to avoid bumping the boys into rocks and other obstacles. The key thing was to keep the boys' full-face masks on—a task that, as the hours passed, became mentally exhausting. One wrong manoeuvre, one wrong turn could dislodge them. If that happened in a section of deep water and there were still 100 or 150 metres left to dive, the diver would have only a matter of minutes to get the boy's head out of the water and into the open air before he drowned. The oxygen saturating the boys' systems would buy them a little extra time, but not much. The reality was that if a face mask came off—depending on where it happened in the cave—it could be impossible to save the boy, and the diver would have to carry a corpse out of the cave. The extra concentration required to protect these young lives would take a heavy toll on the divers.

Volanthen, in his matter of fact way, would later liken bringing out the Boars to carrying a shopping bag. Where a section was narrow and deep, he would hold the boy close to his chest; at other times, when they were swimming through wider, shallow waters he would hold his Boar out to one side and manoeuvre him around any obstacles. Doing so also allowed him to see what lay ahead.

————

In chamber 8, Craig Challen, Claus Rasmussen and Mikko Paasi were enduring an agonising wait as they waited for Mallinson and Note to arrive. But as soon as they reached chamber 8, the trio swung into action. First, Challen checked the child's breathing; he was alive and breathing normally. The three men were flooded with relief.

Now it was time to start removing Note's diving gear. A muddy, rocky section that was about 200 metres long lay ahead and the team would have to carry the boy on a stretcher then drag it through a section that included a narrow sump that was difficult to negotiate. The pumping that had been going on for more than a week had helped drain this section of the cave of most of its water. All of this would have to happen in near darkness, too, with only a few lights to assist the divers as they worked away.

Once they had cleared this section, Challen checked the boy again and the team began to put the kid's diving gear and full-face mask back in place. It was time to go back in the water—another dive, past chamber 7 and through the T-junction and onto chamber 6.

Sometimes the rescuers had to drag the boy after them. Sometimes, at the narrowest points, they would have to try different techniques to get him through sumps and openings that could be as narrow as 40 centimetres. At other times, a steep vertical climb or dip would present itself.

Although each of the boys had lost an average of a little over 2 kilos, it was still difficult to wrangle them through the cave. Every obstacle would eat up precious minutes that raced by. Again and again on that first day it was a case of trial and error as the four British divers grappled with how exactly to get the boys through those first six chambers to chamber 3, where a huge rescue team waited for them. At this point the divers had been working their way into and then back out of the cave for at least four hours.

In chamber 6, about 100 metres past the T-junction, more help was waiting. Like the trio in chamber 8, Ivan Karadzic and Erik Brown had been sitting in the near darkness for about two and a half hours, although to them it seemed much longer. Chamber 6 is about 4 metres high from floor to ceiling, and perhaps 3 metres wide, and at the time the water was about waist deep for an adult. Its muddy banks offered prime real estate for stowing spare air and oxygen tanks for the divers and the boys, and somewhere for the two men to perch while they waited for them to come through. It was hard for Karadzic and Brown to hear each other clearly against the continuous echo of dripping water. They were primed and ready for the moment the first boy and his diver would appear and they could check the Boar's breathing. But as Mallinson surfaced and started swimming with Note towards them, the two men were consumed by one fundamental question—was the boy still alive?

They had to face this moment over and over again, as each boy was brought into chamber 6. Had some terrible mishap occurred? Was the diver bringing a dead child towards them? They simply couldn't know what was coming.

Miraculously, one by one, the boys came through safely and they were all fine.

Brown says he will never forget the moment when the first boy came through: 'You're not sure what's about to happen, but you're optimistic. You're on edge, in the dark, and you finally see that little light appear. Your heart is going a million miles a minute. When they came through the darkness, that first time, it was in slow motion.'

So difficult were the conditions in the dark chamber, and so great was the pressure of those hurried minutes to check each boy, that Brown and Karadzic never knew which boys were coming through, or in what order. And it wouldn't be until they themselves had reached the entrance at the end of the day before they learnt if the boy they had just helped through their section of the cave had managed to survive all the way.

Karadzic describes the job he and Brown did like this: 'The divers could change their own tanks, but the kids couldn't obviously. So we would take charge of the kids, to give the diver a short break. At this point, they had been diving for two hours with the kid. So every minute where they didn't have to worry about someone else's life was probably beneficial. They got a five-minute break.'

Then the pair would spend perhaps five more minutes making sure the boy's mask was properly fitted, and that there were no leaks in the equipment. If another injection of a sedative was required, they would deal with that, too. And, finally, with the British diver leading the way, Karadzic and Brown would help swim the boys, one by one, about 300 metres from chamber 6 to chamber 5.

Then the Brit would take charge again—with perhaps a couple more hours of diving ahead of him—and Brown and

Karadzic would return to their station and prepare for the next arrival. 'I don't know if I was scared, but having to deal with the situation, it's obviously not something I've trained for or ever tried,' Karadzic recalls. 'It was fairly stressful, you don't want to do anything wrong. But we were told by the medical team what to do, what to look for, so that's what we did.'

One by one, Mallinson, Volanthen, Jewell and Stanton kept going calmly and methodically—diving through the canals, struggling through the mud and guiding each boy around rocks, through narrow openings, S-bends and sumps, and up rocky slopes.

By the time they reached chamber 3, where they were greeted by about 150 people, the divers were naturally exhausted. But each man would hug his boy before handing him over to the huge support team.

The atmosphere in the chamber was electric, and there was a murmur of excited voices as the rescuers carried out their tasks as quickly and efficiently as they could. Doctors and nurses checked the health of each boy while the Skeds and the pulley system were made ready. Thai, American, Chinese and Australian personnel and more swung into action, helping the divers to get the boys through the final chambers and out to the waiting ambulances.

One by one, the four divers came through, and each time the boy they were escorting arrived alive. Jason Mallinson was the first man out with 15-year-old Prajak 'Note' Sutham. He was followed by, in order, John Volanthen, Chris Jewell and Rick Stanton. The other three boys who came out on that first rescue day were 14-year-old Nattawut 'Tle' Takamrong, 15-year-old Pipat 'Nick' Pho and 17-year-old Peerapat 'Night' Sompiangjai.

The four divers had brought the first four boys to the brink of freedom, defying everyone's expectations as well as the harsh conditions, perhaps Mother Nature herself—or the Princess of the cave. Just four of them, with nine men in support positions along the way, had swum, dived and dragged the boys for hours, through the hardest sections of the cave.

The next day, Monday, they would have to do it all again.

9–10 JULY: INSIDE
Escape to freedom

Narongsak Osatanakorn had predicted that the first news of the rescue operation would not filter out until about 9 pm that evening. He was wrong, by several hours.

That Sunday, as the rescue was underway, all of Thailand seemed to stop; everyone was praying for good news from Tham Luang cave. At the District Administration office, where journalists were working the phones, desperate for the smallest skerrick of information on the Boars' fate, the hours dragged by. Thai volunteers, who for two weeks had worked tirelessly, supporting the rescue effort, kept handing out hundreds of free meals. Coconut ice creams with little flags planted in them were a welcome addition as the hot tropical sun bore down that afternoon. The message on the flag? 'We give moral support to our heroes. Keep fighting!'

At about 4 pm, a relatively short downpour swept through, saturating laptops and cameras that weren't carefully positioned under the tents and reminding everyone that the rescuers were racing against time and the weather.

Then, just after 6 pm, the incredible news began to break on Khao Sod, a local website. The first Boar was out of the cave—and he was alive! The news took off like a rocket, racing through the Administration office and all over Thailand. Could this really be true?

Journalists rushed to confirm the news, and Twitter—as always, a mish-mash of rumours, facts and speculation—went into meltdown.

Soon after, a second boy was said to be out, too. The global news agency Reuters confirmed it.

'Two kids are out. They are currently at the field hospital near the cave,' Tossathep Boonthong, chief of Chiang Rai's health department, told them. 'We are giving them a physical examination. They have not been moved to Chiang Rai Hospital yet.'

But soon after 7 pm, the first ambulance was heard racing towards the hospital.

Later, a rescue helicopter would pass over, headed towards the hospital with another Boar on board.

And then word came through that the third and fourth boys had also been saved. The Thai Navy SEALs' Facebook page, which had been a regular source of information during the weeks the boys had been in the cave, announced: 'Fourth Wild Boar is out at 7.47 pm.' It would eventually emerge that the first three Boars had come out at 5.40 pm, 5.50 pm and 7.30 pm, respectively, but it was only later that their identities—Note, Tle, Nick and Night—would become well known.

Cheers rang out over Thailand.

The parents of the boys were overjoyed, but they didn't yet know which boys had been saved. Some local news outlets began reporting that 13-year-old Mongkol 'Mark' Boonpiam was the first boy out of the cave. He was originally supposed to be one of the six boys rescued on day 1 but, in the end, Mark—one of the smaller boys—was forced to wait until day 3, when he was the last of the Boars to come out of Tham Luang cave.

As 8.30 pm approached, some news outlets—including the usually reliable Reuters—were reporting that the fifth and sixth boars had been freed. The fog of breaking news had descended and, in the scramble for information, some mistakes had been made. 'Four' was the magic number on day 1, and corrections would have to be released.

Just after 9 pm, Narongsak fronted the media in the car park of the Pong Pha Sub District Administration Office. It was a decidedly mundane setting in which to announce some extraordinary news. Although the rescue chief had been out by three hours in predicting when the boys might emerge, he was precise as he announced the details of the first, successful mission.

'We have sent four of them to the hospital, all safe,' he began. 'What's the next plan? We will get ready and make sure that everything is 100 per cent because all of the oxygen tanks and equipment have to be re-filled.'

One of the boys—most likely the one whom Richard Harris had monitored for 30 minutes before his dive began—was not in fantastic condition. But overall, Narongsak said, 'Today's operation is more successful than we expected.'

Ninety divers from around the world, including 40 Thais and 50 international divers, had contributed to the rescue on day 1. In all, thousands of people had contributed to the overall success of the mission.

The next operation would begin in ten to twenty hours—but Narongsak wouldn't say much more than that. He didn't even say which of the boys had been saved. Thai authorities were doing their best to keep firm control of the release of any information about the rescue mission.

———

Day 2 of the rescue began without any media fanfare. The supply of oxygen and air cylinders had been replenished overnight, the equipment had all been checked and the plan was set. So they just did it.

Just after 11 am on Monday morning, 9 July—an hour later than on the first day—thirteen divers re-entered the cave and began the second rescue mission. The teams again left in pairs, about twenty minutes apart, with Craig Challen as Richard Harris's dive buddy. John Volanthen, Rick Stanton, Chris Jewell, Jason Mallinson and Harris reached the boys at Nern Nom Sao. Once again, Challen was stationed in chamber 8, alongside Claus Rasmussen and Mikko Paasi. But the line-up of the rest of the main dive team had changed slightly, as Ivan

Karadzic, the Danish diver, had pulled out due to illness. So in chamber 6 Erik Brown was joined by Jim Warny, who had been in chamber 5 on day 1 of the rescue. In chamber 5, Connor Roe was joined by Josh Bratchley, another member of the British Cave Rescue Council who had joined the rescue mission.

The 'dive out' order was the same as day one—Mallinson would go first, followed by Volanthen, Jewell and Stanton. Each man would bring out one Boar.

The four boys who would come out on Monday were 13-year-old Panumas 'Mick' Sangdee, 14-year-old team captain Duganpet 'Dom' Promtep, 14-year-old Ekarat 'Bew' Wongsukchan and 14-year-old Adul Sam-on, the boy perhaps best known to the world due to that first, stuttering video when the team had been found by Stanton and Volanthen.

Despite the success of day 1, the rescuers were tense; just because the first day had gone smoothly, it did not mean that day 2 would be easier, or even as successful. They were also beginning to feel the effects of the previous day's operation, especially the cumulative effects of so many dives in difficult conditions in such a short space of time. They were burning kilojoules like crazy as their bodies ate up energy. This made the assistance they were given by the SEALs, the US and the Australian teams, who carried heavy equipment such as their oxygen cylinders, invaluable.

Of course, after the 100 per cent success rate on day 1, everyone's expectations had soared. But the conditions in the cave were still treacherous; they still had to negotiate the same tunnels and stretches of murky, underwater passages, and face the same risks posed by the accidental dislodging of a face mask. Nothing about the mission had become easier. As Brown put it, 'Just because we got four out on day 1, didn't mean everything would work on day 2. Day 2 was equally as dangerous, on day 2 we could go zero from four [rescued]. The hardest part was there was no playbook for this.'

For Jewell, the sense of elation at the end of day 1 was quickly replaced by a sense of foreboding: 'There was a sense of euphoria mixed very heavily with a sense that we would have to do this again, not just once, but twice more. We would have to go through [the] entire stressful process, from start to finish, on at least two more occasions. And the diving wasn't going to get any easier.'[1]

————

The fact that the plan had worked on day 1, at least, gave the divers some confidence that they could do it again. In addition, the pumps were still working, preventing the water levels from rising as more rain passed over Doi Nang Non mountain and flowed into Tham Luang cave. And early, unofficial reports from the hospital indicated that, while a couple of the boys had minor ailments, on the whole they were recovering well.

In the days ahead, the boys would play with Lego, playdough and spend time drawing in the hospital, under the watchful eyes of doctors and psychologists.

One of the major shocks the boys would confront, which could have potentially had a significant psychological impact on them, was the death of Saman Gunan. The team learnt of this just a couple of days before they left the cave. They were shocked and saddened that someone had died trying to rescue them.

The whole operation, overseen by the Thai military and with a prominent contribution from the US military personnel on site, was being run in a regimented fashion, which not only suited the disposition of the military types in charge but also helped minimise the risk of misunderstandings and mishaps. Limiting the variables just made sense, and only essential changes were made to the rescue procedure. After all, it was impossible to impose order on either the cave or the weather. Brown, typically self-deprecating, plays down his role in chamber 6 during the rescue mission: 'The UK divers were always in charge and our job was to always support them, "yes sir, no sir", that sort of thing. We had to facilitate whatever they needed.'

By the time they reached chamber 6, the kids were usually okay and their oxygen tanks didn't need changing. But the waypoint did allow the Brits to change over their own cylinders and have a brief respite as two extra sets of hands offered to help pull the boys through.

'Sometimes they would come through and everyone would be fine and no help was needed. Sometimes we would change [a] kid's tanks. There wasn't a routine. It really depended on the situation on day to day, from child to child,' says Brown.

The UK divers were changing tanks more regularly than the boys, because of the amount of effort required to dive themselves out, while also dragging, steering and guiding the boys through the cave. But fewer tanks were used by the divers on day 2, as they became more accustomed to the job at hand.

Towards the end of day 2, after Stanton had come through with the fourth Boar, Harris and Challen appeared. On each of the three rescue days, about fifteen minutes after the last boy was taken from chamber 9, they would dive through to chamber 6 together and pop their heads up to say hello.

But this time it was slightly different. In the middle of one of the most daring rescue missions the world had ever seen, Brown and Harris shared a moment that was extraordinary for its ordinariness. Brown was just sitting in chamber 6, taking it all in, considering the enormity of the whole mission and the role he, personally, was playing. He was also contemplating the dive back to chamber 3 that lay ahead of him: 'I was sitting there [for] ten minutes on day 2.' Then Harris appeared through the darkness from the direction of Nern Nom Sao, on his way out for the night.

'He asked where I was from. I said I was from Canada.' The pair spoke for a few minutes, with Harris asking how the boys were when they had come through chamber 6.

'Four for four,' replied Brown.

'Far out.'

'It was one of those weird moments, a two-minute conversation a mile and a half inside a cave in Thailand,' Brown laughs, struggling to describe what had remained unsaid between the two men in those precious minutes at the end of the second rescue day. 'Dr Harris is an amazing man.'

Then Brown cleared his station, grabbed the empty tanks and started the long dive back. It would be two or three hours before he would know if the day's mission had succeeded. And the four remaining boys and coach Ek would have to spend one more night in the cave.

———

Ever careful to control what the media knew, the Thai authorities didn't breathe a word about rescue day 2 until 3 pm, when Narongsak called the media to another briefing. In essence, the rescue plan was unchanged, he said, and they hoped to repeat the success of day 1. The conditions were as good as they had been on the previous day, and in four to five hours they would know if day 2 had been a success.

The water levels inside the cave were stable, with the pumps still working 24 hours a day to keep water flowing out of Tham Luang and into the nearby fields. Although the downpour the previous afternoon had tested the setup, there was no cause for concern—at least not yet.

The first four boys, meanwhile, had not yet seen their parents; after seventeen days their first, emotional reunion would have to be delayed by a day while the boys underwent exhaustive medical checks. If the results were all positive, then the parents would be able to visit their sons for the first time—although they would have to communicate with them through a wall of glass, as the boys were all in an isolation ward to guard against infection. They had asked, Narongsak added, for Pad Krapow Kai, a spicy Thai stir-fry chicken dish with sweet basil.

Maddeningly, Narongsak still wouldn't confirm which of the boys had come out on day 1. And with that, the briefing was over and the wait for more news from inside Tham Luang cave continued.

Right across the world—from millionaire footballers competing in Russia's World Cup to Australians gathered around their television sets—the rescue had captivated people's attention. The rescue mission cut across cultural boundaries and language barriers, and introduced the majority of the world to the dangerous complexities of caving and cave-diving.

There was something primal and inspiring about rescuers from more than a dozen different nations uniting to try to defeat Mother Nature and save the lives of twelve young boys and their coach from deep inside a dark, deserted cave. Anyone could relate to the basic contours of the story, and just about everyone—at some point in their life—had been afraid of the dark.

In the end, the wait for more news on that Monday afternoon ended sooner than expected. Just before 5 pm, a fifth member of the Wild Boars was seen emerging from the entrance of the cave on a stretcher. Then at 5.15 pm, an ambulance was spotted leaving the cave and heading towards a helicopter that was on standby. A few minutes later the chopper roared away from Mae Sai on its way to Chiang Rai Hospital.

But still no one had confirmed whether the first Boar who had come out was dead or alive. And there was no way to confirm it, given the tight clamp on the dissemination of information. In any event, less than an hour later a sixth boar was seen being treated at the field hospital outside the cave. Boars 7 and 8 followed soon afterwards, with each undergoing a medical check inside the cave, and then again at the field hospital, before being rushed to hospital.

Between 4.45 pm and 7 pm the four boys had emerged— and despite the rescue operation starting an hour later than the day before, it had been completed an hour earlier.

The Thai Navy SEALs, in their trademark style, again marked the moment on their Facebook page: 'Eight Boars in two days. Hooyah!' That trademark cheer, 'Hooyah!', had been heard time and time again around the operation centre outside the cave entrance as the SEALs drilled and prepared for what lay ahead.

Later Narongsak—with a satisfied expression on his face— would begin on a high note as he confirmed the news that was now widely known. 'Today we saved four more. The team is getting used to the operation. In the cave we have more than a hundred staff . . . for guide ropes, to fill tanks and 18 divers to get the kids.'

Throwing another feint to the media, and to the watching world, Narongsak suggested that on Tuesday only another four Boars—the optimum number for the operation—might come out. It didn't ring true; the idea that just one member of the team would be left in the cave—even if it was Ek with Dr Pak and the three brave Thai SEALs who were approaching their ninth day inside—was laughable. His comments seemed to underscore the fact that it was the divers running the rescue plan, not the Thais; Narongsak simply didn't know it yet.

Sitting alongside Narongsak was the deputy commander of the Third Thai Army, Major General Chalongchai Chaiyakham, grinning like the Cheshire Cat as he described how the rescue plan had been 'adapted' and 'sharpened' in the past 24 hours. The number of divers involved in the operation—the great bulk of whom, of course, were in chambers 1 to 3—had grown to more than a hundred on the second day.

'I expect tomorrow will be good news,' Chalongchai said.

But as the second extraordinary rescue day drew to a close, four Boars and their coach remained in the cave that night. Although they had Dr Pak and the SEALs for company, it must have been a very lonely night. By now they knew the four boys from the first day's rescue had made it out safely. But the fate of the second four was still unknown, and they couldn't be sure that the five of them would all make it out safely on the third and final day.

If anything, the result on day 2 was even more extraordinary. The British divers had done it again and saved another four members of the football team, completing the day's rescues in less time than the day before. But could they finish the job with no casualties?

That question would be answered on day 3 of the rescues—Tuesday, 10 July.

In the early hours of 10 July, Elon Musk again attempted to insert himself into the story of the Wild Boars. The tech billionaire announced he had just returned from a visit to the cave. 'Mini-sub is ready if needed. It is made of rocket parts & named Wild Boar after kids' soccer team. Leaving here in case it may be useful in the future. Thailand is so beautiful,' he tweeted.

But in the weeks ahead the billionaire would become increasingly defensive over his 'contribution' to the rescue effort. Responding to a tweet from *BBC World News*, Musk said it was inaccurate to describe Narongsak as the 'rescue chief', and released copies of emails between himself and Richard Stanton that indicated the British diver had encouraged him to keep working on the submarine. 'We're worried about the smallest lad please keep working on the capsule details,' Stanton had written. Moreover, 'based on extensive cave video review & discussion with several divers who know journey, SpaceX engineering is absolutely certain that mini-sub can do entire journey,' Musk added.

Things went downhill from there.

Vern Unsworth, whose extensive knowledge of the cave was a vital component of the cave rescue, criticised Musk's submarine as a PR stunt that had 'absolutely no chance of working' because it couldn't navigate the tight passageways of Tham Luang cave. The billionaire, he added, had been asked to leave very quickly after turning up at the cave.

Musk's subsequent derisive comments about Unsworth were not well received. His contribution, while seen as well-meaning, was also regarded by some observers as a crude attempt to garner some publicity.

Either way, it was a sideshow.

––––––––

Early on Tuesday, 10 July, fog and clouds hung over Doi Nang Non, and it rained incessantly. It wasn't at all clear how much longer the pumps could keep working to hold back the tide. Time was clearly running out for the rescuers. Surely today was the day the final five would come out. Although the rescuers were exhausted, they could now see the finish line. But while preparations were underway for the third and final rescue push, the health of the first eight boys rescued still remained a mystery, and more and more questions were being asked about their condition. None of the families had enjoyed direct contact with their sons yet, and it wasn't even clear if they knew which of the eight boys had been brought out safely.

Narongsak Osatanakorn had initially claimed that the rescued boys were not being named out of respect for the families of the five boys still in the cave. Again, it was a claim that defied belief. At least some of the divers did not know the names of the boys they were bringing out on day 1, and the boys were too sedated to tell them. The boys' nicknames were subsequently written on their hands on days 2 and 3. Nearly 48 hours after the first boys had been rescued some of the parents started to complain publicly about the lack of information from authorities. Somboon Sompiangjai,

Night's father, had complained that, before the first rescue on Sunday, the parents had been told only that the 'strongest children' would come out first.[2] Since then, the information vacuum had continued. 'We have not been told which child has been brought out,' he said. 'We can't visit our boys in hospital because they need to be monitored for 48 hours.'

Finally, the Thai authorities began to respond as the heat was turned up on them by the media publicly. To limit the damage, Dr Jesada Chokedamrongsuk from the Thai Ministry of Public Health was hastily thrust before the cameras.[3] Two of the boys—all of whom remained unnamed— had mild lung infections and signs of pneumonia, she said, while doctors were concerned about the heart rate and body temperature of a third. To protect their eyes after so long in the dark, the boys had worn sunglasses inside for about 24 hours. They would remain in hospital for about a week while their heart rate was monitored and they underwent blood tests and lung X-rays. As a precautionary measure, they would receive IV fluids and vaccines. The boys with slightly abnormal lung X-rays belonged to the first group of Boars but the second group to have been rescued were, if anything, in better shape.

After nine days of energy gels and MREs, all the boys in hospital had started to eat 'normal' food—nothing adventurous, just soft-boiled rice and a small amount of chocolate. Local pork and chicken dishes, and KFC—which the boys had expressed a wish to eat—would come later. Most importantly, the first four boys had seen and spoken to their parents, even though they were in their quarantine ward on the other side of a glass wall, and the second group of four would also see their loved ones later on Tuesday.

But the Thai authorities continued to pressure the families not to speak to the media. Officially, the identity of the first eight Boars who had been rescued from the cave remained a tightly held secret.

10–18 JULY: INSIDE
Mission possible

The news that the eight rescued Boars were in relatively good health boosted the spirits of the rescue team. They needed it. All the divers and rescuers were exhausted. They'd been working a minimum of twelve-hour days, and it was all on 'cave time', as the divers called it. Loosely translated, that meant their days alternated between intense bursts of draining physical activity and long stretches of inactivity, when time would seem to stand still in the dark, damp silence of Tham Luang.

As long as he was in the cave, each man had to constantly maintain a high degree of focus and concentration—when it was time to go, you had better be ready, because a boy's life depended on it. Of course that, too, became wearing after a while.

Moreover, the third day of rescues would ask more of them than the first two days. They had to dive five people out of the cave, not four, and even after they had been taken out of the cave, the rescuers couldn't abandon their stations inside. There were still three Thai SEALs with Dr Pak in Nern Nom Sao.

———

The rescue began at around 11 am on Tuesday, 10 July, while the first details about the rescued Boars were being released. It promised to be a very long day. For the third successive day, the Thais—and, indeed, millions of people around the world—stopped, watched, waited and hoped for the best.

Once again, only minimal changes were made to the rescue plan for the four remaining boys and their coach. All the local and foreign divers and rescuers were expected to follow exactly the same procedure on all three days in order to maintain control, in spite of the chaotic and unpredictable conditions in the cave.

So on day 3 of the rescue, John Volanthen, Rick Stanton, Chris Jewell, Jason Mallinson and Richard Harris swam all the way through to the four remaining Boars and their coach in chamber 9. Jim Warny was moved up again, from chamber 6 to chamber 8, where he joined Craig Challen, Claus Rasmussen and Mikko Paasi.

Mallinson would make the difficult 350-metre dive between chambers 9 and 8 twice.

On his first trip, he would shuttle Coach Ekapol 'Ek' Chantawong to Warny, who would then take over and guide

Ek the rest of the way out. As an adult, Ek would have been more difficult to manoeuvre through the tightest sections of the cave.

The only other notable change was the 'dive out' order. This time, Volanthen would come out first, then Stanton, Jewell and Mallinson last. This meant Mallinson would have extra time to recharge after his first 'shuttle' dive with coach Ek. For his final rescue dive, he was also assigned one of the smaller boys, 13-year-old Mongkol 'Mark' Boonpiam. The other three Boars who would come out on day 3 were 11-year-old Chanin 'Titan' Vibulrungruang, 13-year-old Somepong 'Pong' Jaiwong and 16-year-old Pornchai 'Tee' Kamluang.

The movement of Warny to chamber 8 meant Erik Brown would be flying solo in chamber 6, but it wasn't expected to be a major problem—the divers were using this stop less and less as they became more practised at diving out of the cave. In fact, overall, fewer stops were now required. Finally, Connor Roe and Josh Bratchley would remain in chamber 5.

On that third and final morning, the euphoria of saving eight from eight in the first two days seemed a long time ago. The divers had to be prepared for something to go wrong at any moment. Just because they had now successfully saved eight of the Wild Boars did not mean that day 3 would go off without a hitch. All along, the rescue teams—the Brits and the Americans, the Euro divers, the Thais and the Australians—had expected there to be casualties. But to achieve so much, and then lose someone on the final day, was unthinkable. For all the meticulous planning on the third and final day of the rescue, Tham Luang cave still had the capacity to throw up unexpected difficulties that nearly resulted in catastrophic consequences. By day 3 visibility in some underwater sections of the cave had become abysmal; the mud in other sections had somehow become thicker as the cave floor had dried out. Guidelines and empty cylinders littered the cave, creating more obstacles.

Mallinson would later reveal in an interview with a television reporter that the final dive out was an agony.[1] The face mask intended for young Mark was simply too big for the skinny young Boar and, without a tight seal, he would drown on the way out. Mark had already been sedated with Ketamine, so time was running out.

Another mask, with a different type of seal, was quickly found and pressed onto Mark's face. The strap worked differently, which meant the mask could be dislodged sideways; Mallinson feared that any ill-judged bump could knock it off, and cause Mark to drown. But it was now or never. He pulled the child close to him and began the dive from chamber 9 to chamber 8.

The rescue didn't work out precisely as planned for Jewell, either. Close to the end of his dive out, Jewell lost his grip on the guideline between chamber 4 and chamber 3. In the pitch black of the cave, it was a terrifying moment for the Brit—a brush with death. Keeping one hand on the vulnerable, sedated Boar, Jewell began to search around in the dark for the line that would lead him and his charge to safety. 'I knew the dive line couldn't be far away but I couldn't find it. I deliberately tried to slow my breathing down, tried to stay exactly where

I was, stayed stationary, deploying a strategy of looking for the line and then ultimately finding an electrical cable,' he later revealed in a television interview.[2]

The sense of relief that flooded over him when he found the cable was momentarily overwhelming. But Jewell still needed to get back to safety and take stock of the situation. He was also worried about his boy: hypothermia was a risk after an extended period in the water, despite the wetsuit the boy was wearing. Disoriented, he found his way back to the sand in chamber 4, where he wrapped his Boar in a space blanket and waited for a colleague who could provide a second pair of hands to come by.

Fortunately, Mallinson and Harris were through soon enough, and helped him finish the job. Jewell ended up being the last of the British divers out of the cave on that day—just— with Mallinson pipping him on the way out.

In chamber 3, the tension and excitement was building. One, two, three, four . . . five. The British divers, leaders and heroes all of the rescue, could scarcely believe it. Relief washed over the men. They were all out.

Now the more than 150 people stationed between chamber 3 and the cave exit swung into action. There was a momentary release of exultation that the boys were out, but there was still plenty of work to do.

The kids' breathing still had to be checked: okay.

Doctors rushed over. More checks were made. The plan had always been to keep the boys completely 'under', at least as far as chamber 3. But on the third day at least one of the boys was filmed awake and talking by the time he reached the cave entrance.

One by one, on that Tuesday evening, Ek and each of the boys was placed in a Sked and passed through the hands of many rescue workers. Thai SEALs, Americans, Chinese and Australians formed relay teams, hoisting them up and down the steep, slippery slopes, or dragging and carrying them through the sections between chamber 3 and chamber 2. Closer to the cave's exit, another point where there were still considerable areas of water to negotiate, floats were attached to the Skeds.

Wang Yingjie's team of eleven Chinese rescuers from the Beijing Peaceland Foundation did their part, hauling in equipment and helping to transport the boys through the last few chambers. This team had played a major role in setting up the pulley system that was used to transport the boys part of the way out from chamber 3. However, the boys were carried for much of the way out from chamber 3 and would pass through more than a hundred pairs of hands on their way out, too.[3] Wang says the pulley system was built to support four times the estimated maximum weight of the boys. Designing and installing the system had proved difficult because of the low visibility in the cave, the long distances they were attempting to span, and the twisting, turning nature of the tunnel, which is very narrow at certain points.

'We worked with the Royal Thai Navy, the US, Australia and [the] UK and we were one team,' Wang says. 'Each day we had a meeting and each of us getting [*sic*] an assignment. We would do our part. Language wasn't a barrier and we found that language used in technical terms like diving and rope system[s] was universal. Since the beginning, my goal . . . as a volunteer was to save the kids and we—the whole world—shared the same goal.'

In chamber 2, more pulleys were managed by Thai volunteers, amateur cavers, climbers and rope access technicians from the nearby city of Chiang Mai. Again, these lines helped with transporting the Skeds through some of the trickiest parts of the cave, but much of the carrying work still had to be done by hand. At one point, to facilitate the transport of the boys, each Sked was slid along the huge water-pump hoses.[4]

During the first few days of their involvement, the AFP divers had hauled hundreds and hundreds of kilograms of kit through thick mud and flooded sections of the cave to chamber 3. Now, on the last rescue day, they were in the thick of it, too, helping to carry the boys out of the cave.

'Once [each boy] was handed over to us, we were down at his face mask just listening for that breath,' said Senior Constable Matthew Fitzgerald, remembering the overwhelming relief he felt as each of the boys was found to be still breathing.

Kiwi diver Ross Schnauer, an expat who had lived in Thailand for about fifteen years, was another member of the international contingent who volunteered to help.

On that final day, Schnauer spent about seven hours in the cave helping carry the boys out in difficult conditions.

Working in a team of four and relying on headlights to combat the darkness of the cave, they would receive about five minutes' notice before a boy would arrive.

'When they came out of the water they were put on a stretcher, their oxygen changed and the first aid guys watched them over . . . then we were paired ready to receive them and move them in a chain.'

Coming through his section of the cave, Schnauer noticed that some of the boys had their eyes open while others were unconscious. But he was focused on the mission at hand.

'The part of the cave we were in was very rocky and unstable. You had to be very careful where you put your feet. To be honest, I did not notice anything about the boys, I was too worried about where to put my feet and make sure that I had a tight grip on the legs. You would not let them go at this time.'[5]

The rescue team left the full-face masks on the boys for the rest of the journey out of the cave because the air quality in the cave had declined so severely, and the Boars' cylinders contained higher than usual concentrations of oxygen that would saturate their blood.

As Ek and the final group of boys exited the cave one by one, they were checked at the field hospital outside before they too were bundled into ambulances and ferried to the waiting helicopters, thence to Chiang Rai Hospital.

Back at the car park of the Pong Pha Sub District Administration Office, news that the final five had been successfully rescued leaked out. But this time it took only about twenty minutes. Around an hour later Narongsak Osatanakorn confirmed the mission was under way—and that all five were on their way out. 'Today we might have to wait longer, but it will be worth the wait to get all five out,' he said. Cheers went up among the volunteers and, indeed, across the world.

Heavy rain had fallen earlier in the day, but once it ceased in the early afternoon, the temperature in Mae Sai soared. At 4.06 pm, a little more than five hours after the rescue began, the first Boar—coach Ek—was out of the cave and on his way to hospital. The rest emerged in a rush; an hour later, the last boy was freed.

Just before 7 pm the Thai Navy SEALs, who had once again been providing updates on their Facebook page, announced: '12 wild Boars and coach out of the cave. Everyone safe. This time, waiting to pick up four frogs. Hooyah!' Then: 'We are not sure if this is a miracle, a science, or what. All the thirteen Wild Boars are now out,' they added a little later.

It had taken only eight hours to get all five out, a quicker extraction than on days 1 and 2. Ambulances screamed by, helicopters buzzed overhead. The noise confirmed—as if further confirmation was required—that the last four boys and their coach were on their way to hospital. Safe. Saved. Residents of Chiang Rai, cheering and blowing whistles in support of the Boars and their rescuers, gathered near the hospital where the boys were being cared for.

But there were still four people to come out.

———

While people outside the cave were celebrating the rescue of Ek and the last four boys, those four 'frogs'—Dr Pak and the three SEALs—were still in the cave. And although these men had managed to make the dangerous dive through the cave once before, getting out again was going to be a dangerous exercise for them.

The quartet had gone in nine days earlier. Since then the conditions in the cave had changed markedly: while the water levels had fallen, the amount of mud and debris had increased, creating more obstacles. And unlike the British, Australian and Euro divers, these four men were not experienced cave divers. They had taken hours longer to get through to Nern Nom Sao than the Brits. Since then they'd been sitting in the dark for nine days, eating ration packs and caring for twelve scared kids and a young coach as they concentrated on the Boars' welfare rather than their own. The dangers were very real. Time passed without any word that Dr Pak and the three SEALs had made it out of the cave, and it slowly dawned on people that the 'four frogs' might be at risk, too.

In the end, the four men emerged almost two and a half hours after the last boy. When the final SEAL arrived in chamber 3 from Nern Nom Sao, he was greeted with a roar of celebration; the atmosphere was electric with a shared sense of relief. The SEALs had not forgotten Saman Gunan, one of their brothers, but now, finally, everyone else was safe.

One of the AFP divers vividly remembers that roar, which bounced off the walls from chamber 3 all the way to the entrance. 'I was right down the bottom [near the entrance] but you could hear all the cheers,' he says. 'It was like a Mexican wave when we got the last diver out, that's when the cheers and shouting happened.'

However, their rescue wasn't officially confirmed until fifteen minutes into Narongsak Osatanakorn's press conference that Tuesday evening. Of course the Thai Navy SEALs captured the moment for posterity; a photo of the quartet—dressed all in black, with sunglasses, face masks and diving kit hanging off them, giving the camera the thumbs up—quickly went viral.

Wang Yingjie, from the Chinese Beijing Peaceland Foundation contingent, said that many people had thought the rescue mission was over once the boys were out. 'At that moment, our focus was on [the] SEALs because all the kids were brought out and we were pretty sure they would be safe.' But when the four men finally emerged from the cave, 'we realised that it was over and the whole world knew it. We were overjoyed but we never expected that we would lose our fellow rescue worker [Saman Gunan]. Some people might ask why we were sad, I'd say that he was one of the team and we were "one".'

But Tham Luang cave had one more surprise for the rescuers.

Just as the pressure was finally easing, now that all the Wild Boars and their companions in chamber 9 had been rescued, the unthinkable happened. The pumps, which had held back the water levels in Tham Luang cave for more than a week, began to fail.

Erik Brown, who at the time was with his dive buddies Claus Rasmussen and Mikko Paasi in chamber 3, vividly remembers the moment the pumps failed: 'We were sitting there, and we said we would wait until everyone leaves. We waited for nearly three hours [for the final four] in chamber 3.

'Those pumps had been working for like seven days straight. It was right before the first SEAL popped his head out. There was a loud bang. Then, as number 3 comes out, a second pump breaks. The water level was now rising fast; you [could] see the water level rising. We had all our dive gear sitting there, we just had to leave it.'

At this stage there were perhaps 30 people—divers, Thai Navy SEALs, US Marines—still in chamber 3. Overall, there were about a hundred rescue workers between that chamber and the entrance. They were all being chased out of Tham Luang cave by a wall of water.

Closer to the entrance, the AFP divers were involved in a half-hearted clean-up when they heard the pumps fail, but didn't immediately realise what had happened until rescuers, their headlights glinting in the dark of Tham Luang, suddenly appeared, running towards them.[6]

'There were a hundred guys running down the hill and the water was coming . . . [it] was noticeably rising,' one of the AFP divers says. He and his colleagues simply turned and ran.

Miraculously, everyone got out, but it was a final reminder of the power of Mother Nature and just how narrowly they had all escaped disaster.

Back at the Pong Pha Sub District Office, Narongsak Osatanakorn was in full swing. The operation had been a role model for the world—this truly global effort, which in the end had included some 10,000 people, including a hundred divers, had succeeded. They had made 'Mission Impossible' possible, he said.

After eighteen days, it was done.

———

Wednesday, 11 July, dawned like any other in Mae Sai. It was mid-summer, warm, and the threat of rain hung heavy in the air. But it was no ordinary day in this sleepy border town in the far north of Thailand.

Overnight, as the thirteen Wild Boars were re-united in Chiang Rai Hospital and the rescuers gathered to celebrate, praise from both world leaders and ordinary citizens, all over the world, had poured out on social media. Cartoons, photos, videos and memes were shared as people celebrated their delight that the boys had been saved.

Iceland's prime minister, Katrín Jakobsdóttir, was the first world leader to offer her congratulations: 'Today, hope, compassion, and courage has won. Warmest wishes for a speedy recovery to all of you brave boys from your friends in Iceland.'

Donald Trump got in on the action, too: 'On behalf of the United States, congratulations to the Thai Navy SEALs and all on the successful rescue of the twelve boys and their coach from the treacherous cave in Thailand. Such a beautiful moment—all freed, great job.'

The Spanish royal family and Bhutan's prime minister, Tshering Tobgay, joined the rush to fete the boys and their rescuers.

And that Tuesday evening Prime Minister Malcolm Turnbull called the Australian team on the ground and told them they had 'inspired the world, you've inspired the nation'. He singled out Dr Richard Harris as one of the heroes of Tham Luang cave.

But Harris, in trademark fashion, deflected the praise: 'The big heroes in this are the children and the Thai Navy SEALs who were looking after them. They were the toughest blokes and kids I've ever had the privilege to meet.

'They were the ones responsible for their own morale and really their own safety and without them being in the state they were in, we couldn't have done anything. So that's where all the credit lies, really.'

Turnbull also offered Harris his condolences on behalf of the nation. Tragically, on Tuesday evening, as the doctor had emerged from the cave for the last time, his father had died at home, thousands of kilometres away in Adelaide. Of course, those private moments between Turnbull and the Australian team didn't last long; soon after, the prime minister posted a video recording of the Skype chat to Twitter.

For the Thai military junta, struggling to unite a divided nation after the most recent military coup, the PR value of the rescue was priceless.

And of course the Thai SEALs chimed in again on their Facebook page:

> Appreciate great help from all teams—divers from
> all over the world, medic teams, several ex-SEALs,

supporting teams, Kruba Boonchum and other spiritual teams, great kitchen teams, oxygen refuelling team, water management team, electricity team, mountain climbing team . . . Mae Sai people, and people from all corners of the world.

Today the united force of humanity is at work. The world will never forget this rescue mission.

The SEALs had summed it up better than any politician could.

———

But away from the cameras and the attention-seeking politicians, desperate to bask in the reflected glory of the successful rescue mission, the Boars were still in hospital. Later that morning an official from Thailand's Ministry of Public Health gave another update on the condition of the boys.

It was more good news. The final five Boars, including their coach, were fine; physically and mentally, they were in good shape. The doctors were no longer concerned about the health of the boys who had shown signs of pneumonia on the first day of the rescue; antibiotics would take care of any lingering symptoms.

The first four Boars had now been reunited with their families, and the second group of four—the authorities had still not released their names—would see their parents later that day.

Also on Wednesday, at a press conference held by rescue mission chief Narongsak Osatanakorn and medical officers, Thai authorities released footage of Ek and the twelve boys in their beds in the Chiang Rai Hospital. The video drove home the impact of those eighteen days in the cave on the boys and their families, who had waited and hoped against all the odds that they would see their sons again. While all the boys were becoming stronger, some still looked painfully thin. With green surgical masks covering their mouths and noses, the boys can be seen talking to doctors and nurses, and making short statements that begin with '*Wai*', the traditional Thai greeting, their hands pressed together as if in prayer. A couple of the boys make the 'V for victory' sign, and Bew, joking, raises his fists in victory. Slow-cooked pork with steamed rice, crispy fried pork, steak and KFC are among the foods the boys want to eat, they tell an off-camera questioner while their mothers and fathers, watching through the glass, wave at their sons and cry.

Narongsak said the boys were neither heroes nor villains— the real heroes were the rescuers. 'They are children being children, it was an accident.'

The Wild Boars, who had been offered free tickets to the World Cup final by the International Federation of Association Football (FIFA), would not be able to fly to Russia. In any case, coach Ek and three of the boys were stateless and had no passport. And they couldn't even watch the game live because it was broadcast quite late in Thailand and the doctors were determined they should have plenty of rest.

Some of the divers involved in the rescue came to the hospital to meet the boys whom they had saved. Dozens of the world game's biggest stars had tweeted their congratulations, and now invitations to visit clubs as illustrious as Manchester United and FC Barcelona flooded in. There was even talk of movie deals.

Meanwhile, the medical checks, tests and vaccinations would continue for the boys for a month or so longer. As they were gradually re-introduced to 'real' food, they slowly regained their strength. They wouldn't be allowed to leave the hospital for another week, as the doctors—and the Thai regime—were terrified that something would still go wrong.

On 18 July, a week and a day after coach Ek and the last four boys had been rescued, the Wild Boars appeared before the cameras for the first time since that second, short video of them in hospital had emerged after they had left the cave. It was a carefully controlled event: all the questions had been submitted to the government beforehand and then screened by psychologists.

They would be able to go home in a week. Then on 25 July, eleven of the twelve boys (Adul is a Christian) would be ordained as Buddhist novices—a common practice in Thailand—for eleven days. Coach Ek would resume the life of a monk for three months. It was a way of showing thanks, and of honouring the memory of Sergeant Saman Gunan.

As Ek put it, 'the only thing we could do [to acknowledge Saman's sacrifice] was to enter the monkhood. Becoming a monk was to repay [the] kindness and sacrifice from everyone in this operation.'

As they all filed on stage, wearing new, freshly pressed Wild Boar uniforms, the contrast with their physical appearance even a week before was stark. Their cheeks were plumper, their faces wreathed in smiles, and they all sported fresh haircuts. After mugging for the cameras with some footballs, the boys sat down with two child psychologists, and with Dr Pak and the three SEALs who had been in the cave with them, to respond to questions the world wanted answered.

Among the hundreds of people in the audience, many of the boys' school friends cheered them on as they continued to charm the world. One by one, they introduced themselves again.

'Hi, my name is Ek.'

'Hi, my name is Tee.'

'Hi, my name is Adul.'

And so on.

Slowly, they recounted the moment they went into the cave. How they had survived by drinking the dripping water, tried to dig their way out of Nern Nom Sao, and how they had grown weaker each day, all the while continuing to urge each other on until the dramatic turning point when the two British divers arrived, and they had conversed with them in clipped English.

Ek and Adul, two of the more confident members of the team, answered most of the questions. Young Mark revealed how scared he had felt when they couldn't go home—and how worried he was that his mother would scold him. Bew recalled how, whenever one of them felt down and started to feel their situation was hopeless, he had told his brother Boars to keep fighting.

'I think we felt like we are the same family, because the Navy SEALs have taken care of us as if we were in their family. We ate together, we slept together,' Ek said.

'I felt like he is my father, because he called us sons,' Mark added, referring to Dr Pak.

As the event wrapped up, one by one the boys shared their dreams for the future. Most said they wanted to be professional footballers, or Thai Navy SEALs, or both. A couple of the older boys added they also wanted to go to university and get a good education. All of them wanted to make their parents proud.

EPILOGUE

The seven Brits looked like any other group of middle-aged holiday-makers returning from a warmer climate. Wearing shorts and T-shirts and looking tired, the returning divers spoke to reporters at London's Heathrow Airport as jets roared overhead.

Rick Stanton, as always, led off. The divers, he said, weren't heroes. 'This was completely uncharted, unprecedented territory and nothing like this has been done [before]. So, of course there were doubts. I knew that we had a good team, with good support from the Thai authorities, the caving community and rescue organisations, so we had the best we could to make a plan work.

'There was a lot of chaos but we were so task oriented that we blanked that out and carried on with the task at hand until we achieved success.

'Are we heroes? No, we are just using a very unique skill set which we normally use for our own interests and sometimes we give back to the community.' This was Stanton, who famously disliked talking to the media, to a tee—brusque, modest, brushing aside questions about the details of the boys' sedation.

Chris Jewell allowed himself a little more emotion as he spoke of the extremely challenging conditions in which they had worked, and of the awful burden of being responsible for saving the life of another human being. 'We are delighted for the successful outcome. We played a part in an international effort.'

Despite their protestations that they were not heroes, on 24 July they attended a reception at 10 Downing Street hosted by the British prime minister, Theresa May.

Back in Thailand, on the same day, Thai authorities promised that the four stateless Boars—coach Ek, Mark, Adul and Tee—would be given legal assistance to secure Thai citizenship. The process would be finished within six months, they said. Narongsak Osatanakorn had predicted the four stateless Boars would grow up to be great Thai citizens, but now cautioned that everything would have to proceed according to the laws of the land.

Of course, the process was fast-tracked; by 8 August, the four stateless Boars had been granted citizenship of Thailand. The whole episode had highlighted, if only for a moment, the plight of the hundreds of thousands of other stateless people who live in the border regions of Thailand, Myanmar and Laos.

Life began to return to normal for the boys. After their time living as novice monks, they went back to school. The teachers instructed the boys' friends to treat them as if nothing had changed, and not to ask them about what had happened in the cave. But of course that was never going to happen.

Seventeen-year-old Auttaporn Khamheng, a friend of Dom's who had volunteered for the rescue effort, was delighted to have his buddy back. 'I don't ask anything about that because many people ask him. I don't want to bother him at all. Also, there are some people that are jealous and gossip about him. I do worry that Dom might get annoyed because so many people ask about the cave. That's why I don't ask anything.'

Football was still on hold for the Boars, however. They had more than a month of schoolwork to catch up on, and that took priority.

The cave rescue had shone a light on the tiny little Mae Sai Prasitsart school, too. Ordinarily, the bigger schools in Chiang Rai Province are the first to be offered the chance to take their sports players on overseas football trips. This year, Auttaporn says, Mae Sai Prasitsart was invited to take some of its footballers on an exchange trip to Japan.

In the Mae Sai district, farmers who had seen their crops destroyed when millions of litres of water from the Tham Luang cave flooded their fields were beginning to pick up the pieces again. Thai authorities had offered the farmers financial compensation, which would make a difference but, even so, local men and women like Noy Kerdkaew felt no bitterness about the loss of their crops as long as it helped get the boys out.

'I can always grow again, but life cannot,' Kerdkew said in an interview a couple of days after the boys were rescued.[1] Like generations before her, she knows the story of the Princess and the cave very well. Whether she completely believes the legend or not, it still has meaning for her and the other locals who live in the shadow of Doi Nang Non. The water that had flowed from the cave onto her farmland, destroying her crops, was the blood of the Princess. And although she had taken Saman Gunan from them, the Princess had let those thirteen boys go.

———

Finally, Richard 'Harry' Harris was heading home. It was Friday, 13 July, and he was sitting in an RAAF C-17 alongside his great mate Craig Challen and Australian police and army divers who had worked to save the Wild Boars in Tham Luang cave. Acclaimed as one of the heroes of the rescue mission, since then the Australian anaesthetist and cave diver had barely had a moment to himself, even to grieve for his father who had died three days before. Two days earlier, while police divers and foreign affairs officials buzzed around outside Mae Sai's Wang Thong Hotel, off Phahonyothin Road, high-fiving and congratulating each other, the Adelaide-based doctor, looking exhausted and lost, had hung back in the face of all the adulation and gratitude of the Thai people and, indeed, the world. Harry's dive buddy, Craig Challen, hovered calmly nearby, frequently grinning. The pair were being positioned for photos, but Harris was lost in his own thoughts, grieving for his father, and wary of all the attention.

Left slightly, now right, now go.

Cameras snapped again and again as different groups arrayed themselves; first, the entire Australian team, then Harris alone; the police and army divers, then Harris and Challen with the foreign affairs staff.

Snap, snap, snap, smartphones at the ready.

DFAT staff, who moments earlier had been snapping selfies, stepped in to try and stop the handful of journalists from taking photos of Harris and Challen. The anaesthetist could not have failed to notice the huge amount of global interest in him, or his part in the incredible story of the Great Cave Rescue. Social media websites such as Twitter and Facebook were awash with people rushing to praise and thank the self-effacing doctor and his retired vet dive buddy from Perth. Everyone wanted to speak to them, from the Australian prime minister down.

I approached Harry for a quick chat and a couple of questions. But what do you say to a man who has just thrilled the world, but lost his father—*Harry, I'm so sorry for your loss. I was wondering, could you spare us five minutes for a chat?*

Instead I asked him, 'Could you just give us an idea of what was going on inside the cave?'

'I can't talk about it, I'm sorry.'

'Please, just one line?' I added hopelessly.

The corner of his eyes hinted, just for a moment, at what the man must have been going through. 'I know people want to know about it, but I'll leave it with these guys,' Harris said, gesturing to the over-anxious DFAT staff. His reluctance to be interviewed, and his exhaustion, were understandable. Media requests were low on his list of priorities, and would remain so. As a friend of his put it: 'They are not your standard talent—not egotistical, money is not a concern, not interested in being famous.'

But on that plane flight home—the first opportunity for Harris to stop and reflect on the extraordinary events at Tham Luang—he opened up a bit in a Facebook post. The doctor sang the praises of the 'awesome foursome'—British divers John Volanthen and Rick Stanton, who had found the missing boys on the night of Monday, 2 July, as well their compatriots Jason Mallinson and Chris Jewell. These four men had swum the boys to safety a week later.

'The efforts and skill of these guys in blazing this trail cannot be underestimated,' he said. 'Following someone else's line is very much easier than finding your own way.'

He also heaped praise on the Thai Navy SEALs, the Thai authorities and the international community for the extra-ordinary rescue effort: 'I have never seen anything like it, man battling to control the natural forces of the monsoon waters.' He also praised the effort to sustain the boys, as well as Dr Pak and the SEALs, who had volunteered to stay inside the cave with them until they were rescued.

In his typical self-effacing style, Harris concluded with a long list of thank-yous and humbly played down his role, and Challen's, in the rescue. 'Craig and I have had a spotlight on our efforts and we want to make everyone realise that while we might have become the face of this rescue for some reason, everyone should know that the role we played was no more or less important than all the many hundreds (perhaps thousands) of people I have mentioned. The part we played has been made out to be a lot more noble than it actually was. We just consider ourselves lucky to have had some skills that we could contribute to the wonderful outcome.'

But if Harris thought that post would be enough, and he could slip quietly back into his ordinary life, he was sorely mistaken. A few days later, along with Challen and the AFP and Navy divers, he was in Canberra to receive the Star of Courage and the Medal of the Order of Australia. Speaking reluctantly after the ceremony, Harris allowed that: 'Frankly, and I think a lot of people have said that, none of us expected those boys to come out, certainly not in the time frame that they did.

'We went cave diving for a few days and we were able to get those kids out.

'I'm just trying to emphasise how big a part so many people played in this. We are not quite sure why the spotlight has shone on us as a pair. It's all quite exciting but I just need to get back to work actually and stop my head swelling and start to relax again.'

Challen's assessment of the dangers posed by the rescue mission was blunt: 'We can handle ourselves in that environ-ment, that's all right, but I just can't stress [enough] how bleak the outlook was for those kids in there. [We are] just overjoyed that it all worked out okay because it could easily have not.'

A few days later, in his home city of Adelaide, Harris was welcomed at a reception hosted by Governor Hieu Van Le at South Australia's Government House. Life would never quite be the same again for Richard Harris, one of the heroes of Tham Luang cave.

A month later Challen, Harris and their buddies in the Wet Mules diving club got together for another dive. Their destination was one of the longest underwater caves in Australia—Tank Cave, near the South Australian town of Mount Gambier. In what was probably a first, a team of local ABC journalists came along to record the Wet Mules' dive for multimedia posterity.

Challen was happy to wax lyrical about their big adventure now it was over, saying 'we're getting back to normal life' but refusing to explain the attraction of cave diving: 'if you need to ask that question, you wouldn't understand the answer.'[2]

But Harris, true to form and in keeping with his decision to decline dozens of requests to participate in newspaper and TV interviews, books and more, said nothing. His deeds in Tham Luang, weeks earlier, would speak for themselves.

———

The road that leads to Tham Luang cave has seen better days. It's easy to speed past it, too, when you're rocketing up Phahonyothin Road on the way into Mae Sai, especially if you don't know what you're looking for.

A small brown wooden sign, set back from the road and framed by rock, announces the entrance to the forest park.

The broken bitumen takes you past fields of bananas and strawberries, some cows and a few lonely farmhouses, set back from the road.

After a couple of kilometres of twists, turns and bumps, an even smaller sign, announcing the entrance to Tham Luang, appears at a turn-off to a dirt road. It's so remote—and apparently, the sprawling Mountain of the Sleeping Lady is so unremarkable—that at the time of writing even Google's all-seeing street-view cameras haven't photographed the final 550 metres of dirt road that lead to the cave entrance (the last drive-by visit was in April 2012). But a month after the rescue of the Wild Boars and their coach, cars still jam the road that leads to the cave. It's Monday, 12 August, the day following Mother's Day, and Thais are enjoying a three-day weekend.

One by one, hundreds of tourists are walking up the dirt road to the entrance of Tham Luang cave, then clambering up and down the staircase that leads to the cave mouth where mud squelches underfoot.

Jeerachayon Arginpat, 31, says he has driven the 250 kilometres from Chiang Mai today with friends and family and that, like many northern Thais, he believes that something sacred protects this site and that, yes, he prayed to the Lady today. 'I just wanted to tell her that we are here to visit and pay respect to her because this is her place and if I do something wrong by mistake, she might forgive us.'

He admits that the rescue was a sort of miracle, as well as the result of good science and engineering. 'I think it might be both, because of luck and also the good management. At first,

I wondered why the rescue mission was so slow. "Just dive and bring them out" . . . but I didn't know the condition inside of the cave. After that, after I knew about the inside of the cave from the media, that's why I think a part of it is quite like a miracle as well.'

Like millions of Thais, and people all over the world, Arginpat had closely followed the news of the rescue every day. And now he was at the cave because 'to be frank, I want to see the rescue scene myself'.

Italian couple Marco Leso and Stella Bortolo, from Milan, have made the trek to Tham Luang for the same reason as Arginpat and his family. They just wanted to see it for themselves and, after planning a 21-day trip to Thailand that would take them through Chiang Mai and the resort island of Koh Samui, they added Tham Luang cave to their list of destinations.

'We watched it at home on Sky and I thought it was a miracle, the story of the boys in the cave,' Bortolo says. 'So we decided just to come here to see it for ourselves. We hope this story is translated into Italian. Everyone wants to know it.'

There are no answers, at least not yet, to be found at Tham Luang cave itself about how those extraordinary eighteen days came about. There is just the silent Princess, the Lady of the mountain, and a blocked cave entrance. Candles flicker, and the air is thick with the smell of burning incense in an unlikely looking brick shrine, where three female mannequins, all dressed in various shades of pink, stand. On the wall behind them hangs another pink dress while bottles of unopened water and figurines sit at their feet. To westerners it might look a bit absurd, but this is deadly serious. Silently, visitors stand palms together in the universally recognised symbol of prayer. In an age when the young think nothing of taking a selfie at a Holocaust memorial, here even the click of a smartphone camera is unusual. No one laughs and chit-chat is kept to a minimum. Visitors linger for up to five minutes, then walk up to the green fence that bars the way into the cave, turn and leave.

A couple of food stalls do a brisk trade, but some more enterprising souls, selling lottery tickets in this place of great fortune, are mostly idle. The visitors are lost in the moment, transfixed by the shrine that honours the Princess. It's as if they can still scarcely believe the boys managed to escape, and they have to see the entrance themselves to believe it.

———

A month earlier, at the top of the road that leads to the cave entrance, this site had swarmed with thousands of people who churned the soaked ground into thick mud as rescuers raced to devise a plan and journalists competed to file updates.

The central square, adjacent to the toilet block, which had been home to hundreds of international media personnel, has been closed off, and work to build a new structure to memorialise the site is underway.

The rows of food stalls staffed by cheerful locals, who handed out free meals, drinks, medical supplies and even underpants for eighteen hours a day are gone.

Further up the hill, a patch of dirt where thirteen ambulances assembled every day, ready to rush the boys to hospital once the rescue mission finally began, is empty.

And the large screened-off camps, where Thai Navy SEALs and a huge cohort of international divers had assembled their diving gear and gathered their cylinders and discussed rescue plans for days on end, have now all been cleared.

Tham Luang is silent, but it will not forget those fateful eighteen days when the Wild Boars were imprisoned in Nern Nom Sao.

The former governor of Chiang Rai Province, Narongsak Osatanakorn—who remained in charge of the rescue mission, even after his governorship expired—has predicted the site will become a living museum. Some of the tools and clothing used in the rescue have already been set aside for a planned future display, and there is talk that a sculpture of Saman Gunan, the retired SEAL who died during the lead-up to the rescue, will also be placed on the site. But even without those keepsakes and mementos, even without a fancy visitors' centre, Tham Luang has already changed forever. It's now a shrine.

ACKNOWLEDGEMENTS

No book has ever arrived as an orphan. This one is no exception.

It has been based on dozens of interviews and extensive research of an extraordinary situation—a highly charged, tense and unprecedented rescue mission carried out in just eighteen days.

Though every effort has been made to ensure accuracy, on occasion, due to the vagaries of human memory, conflicting accounts may emerge.

To Elizabeth Weiss, first of all, for asking me to write it. And for then backing me 100 per cent of the time, taking every phone call and responding to every email and supporting me every step of the way with patience and good advice.

To Angela Handley, a terrific editor who did the same and more, including checking all the tiny details.

To Sarah Baker, for ploughing through my rough first draft and making some sense of it.

To Isabelle O'Brien, for doing such a stellar job in getting this book out there into the world.

And to everyone else at Allen & Unwin, thank you.

To Veena Thoopkrajae, my translator, researcher, eyes and ears on the ground and fellow journalist, who answered every WhatsApp question, day or night, and went the extra mile, I could not have done it without you.

To Akkarawat 'Art' Taokwang, my other translator and researcher, who answered my call on day 1 and was there from start to finish, always with good humour, thank you.

To Martin Ellis, for answering every question with good grace and facts, thank you.

To Bill Whitehouse, Ivan Karadzic, Erik Brown, Dr Pak, Mr Lak, Narongsak Osatanakorn, the parents, boys, friends, teachers and everyone else we spoke to, thank you.

At *The Sydney Morning Herald* and *The Age*, first of all, thanks to Kate Geraghty, one of the world's best photographers. Your brilliant work and good humour in those long days at the cave were amazing.

To Peter Hartcher, my mentor these last five years, who kept an eye on me every step of the way in Canberra and has always been available since I left for Jakarta—including during the writing of this book—thank you.

To Michael Bachelard, James Chessell, Tory Maguire, Lisa Davies and Alex Lavelle, for all thinking I was crazy to take on this book, but backing me to do it anyway, thank you.

ACKNOWLEDGEMENTS

To my colleagues in the Sydney and Melbourne newsrooms who kept me sane, and filing, through all those days at the cave: Lia Timson, Chris Short, Chris Zappone, Ying Xiang Tan, Liam Phelan, Selma Milovanovic, Rachel Olding, Jillian McClelland, Alison Cassar, Nerida Hodgkins, Cosima Marriner, Lucy Rickard, Maher Mughrabi, Steve Jacobs, Aparna Khopkar, Michelle Griffin, Kathryn Wicks, Rachel Clun, Josh Dye, Fleta Page and Marissa Calligeros—thank you.

Thank you also to Amanda Hodge, Michael Safi, Jacob Goldberg, Dan Sutton, Philip Sherwell, Omar Dabbagh, Nicci Smith, Phil Hemingway, Chris Reason, Peter Southwell and Andrew Gordon—brothers- and sisters-in-arms at the cave— and every other reporter who was slogging through it.

To Matthew Holzer, Victor Violante, Rachel Obradovic, Leigh Obradovic, Chris Newcombe, Ralph Carolan, Andrew Carter, Luke James, Charlotte Harper, Eliza Harvey, Adam Harvey, Graham Crouch, Jewel Topsfield, Tom Carolan, David Lipson, Amilia Rosa, Karuni Rompies and Demons Group Therapy, thank you for checking in on me to see that I was getting the job done.

To Ginese Triaca Aldo Massola, Linda Massola and my sister Dr Cate Massola, thank you for inspiring me (and thank you for reading an early draft, too, Cate).

Thanks to my Mum, Rose, my Dad, Carlo, and my stepmum, Carolynn, for taking my calls when I was fed up and didn't think I could finish it.

Most of all, thank you—and all of my love—to my superstar journalist wife, Karen Barlow, who is also a selfless mother extraordinaire who wrangled three kids under two-and-a-half while I wrote fourteen hours a day. Your early feedback on where the draft manuscript was going wrong and where it was going right was invaluable. Your love and belief throughout meant even more.

This book is dedicated to the twelve Wild Boars and their coach, to the men and woman who rescued them, and most of all to Saman Gunan.

Rest in Peace.

REFERENCES

In addition to dozens of interviews with some of the key players involved in the Thai cave rescue, this book has also made use of publicly available reported material from press conferences and speeches.

The sources relied on include my own work for *The Sydney Morning Herald* and *The Age*, plus material from Khaosod English, *The Guardian*, Channel News Asia, *The New York Times*, *The Australian*, News.com.au, *Straits Times*, the BBC, *Bangkok Post*, *The Nation*, CNN, Reuters and other news outlets. The book has also made use of materials in interviews conducted by ABC Australia's Four Corners documentary *Out of the Dark*, Channel News Asia's *Against the Elements*, CNN's *The Miraculous Story of the Thai Cave Rescue* and various interviews with ABC America, BBC, Channel 4 and Channel 5 in the UK.

NOTES

AN ORDINARY DAY IN MAE SAI

1 About AU$1.70, US$1.20.
2 Liam Cochrane, 'Thai cave rescue: "Tham Luang" a magnet for teen adventurers, local man says', ABC Australia, 5 July 2018, www.abc.net.au/news/2018-07-05/thailands-royal-cave-a-magnet-for-teen-adventurers/9946148.
3 See, for example, https://tradingeconomics.com/thailand/wages; 165,000 baht converts roughly to AU$7050 and US$5100.

A RISING SENSE OF DREAD

1 James Longman, 'Exclusive Thai cave rescue interview: Boys' soccer team, coaches on harrowing experience', ABC News America, 23 August 2018, www.youtube.com/watch?v=Jw0_5UlFwHA&t=2s.

SOUND THE ALARM

1 Rebecca Wright and Hilary Clarke, 'British diver recalls Thai cave rescue: "Are we heroes? No"', CNN, 13 July 2018, https://edition.cnn.com/2018/07/13/uk/thai-cave-rescue-british-divers-intl/index.html.

2 About AU$20 to $40, US$15 to $30.

3 Wright and Clarke, 'British diver recalls Thai cave rescue'.

4 Channel News Asia, *Against the Elements*, www.channelnewsasia.com/news/video-on-demand/against-the-elements/against-the-elements-10600394.

5 Chayut Setboonsarng, 'Rescuers to drill hole in Thai cave in hunt for missing boys', Reuters, 28 June 2018, www.yahoo.com/news/rescue-teams-battle-high-water-boys-missing-thai-022041622--sow.html.

6 Piyaporn Wongruang, 'Unknown danger in Thailand's caves', *The Nation*, 21 July 2018, www.nationmultimedia.com/detail/big_read/30350523.

7 'Notes on the Tham Luang survey', Caves & Caving in Thailand (website), undated, www.thailandcaves.shepton.org.uk/luang-survey-notes.

8 Wongruang, 'Unknown danger in Thailand's caves'.

9 James McCarthy, 'Elite Welsh divers' desperate 10-day bid to rescue pal ends in tragedy', *Wales Online*, 14 November 2010, www.walesonline.co.uk/news/wales-news/elite-welsh-divers-desperate-10-day-1885639.

10 Jeffrey Gallant, 'Longest cave penetration dive [DPV]', Diving Almanac (website), 5 April 2017, http://divingalmanac.com/longest-cave-penetration-dive-dpv/.

11 Tek Camp (website), www.tekcamp.co.uk/next-guests.php.

12 Karla Adam, 'Meet the British "A-team" divers at the center of Thailand cave rescue', *Washington Post*, 3 July 2018, www.washingtonpost.com/news/worldviews/wp/2018/07/03/meet-the-british-a-team-divers-at-the-center-of-thailand-cave-rescue/?utm_term=.062b313c7996.

13 Kaweewit Kaewjinda, 'Hapless helpers recount own rescue by divers from Thai cave', *Washington Post*, 26 September 2018, www.washingtonpost.com/world/asia_pacific/hapless-helpers-recount-own-rescue-by-divers-from-thai-cave/2018/09/26/d4c778e4-c191-11e8-9451-e878f96be19b_story.html?utm_term=.3940988b0d80;

Tony Brocklebank, 'British cave divers also rescued four trapped Thai rescuers in Tham Luang Cave', Darkness Below (website), 24 September 2018, https://darknessbelow.co.uk/breaking-news-british-cave-divers-also-rescued-four-trapped-thai-rescuers-in-tham-luang-cave/.

14 Kaweewit Kaewjinda, 'Hapless helpers recount own rescue by divers from Thai cave'.

IN THE DARK

1 Andrew Alan Johnson, 'Inside the sacred danger of Thailand's caves', *The Conversation*, 10 July 2018, https://theconversation.com/inside-the-sacred-danger-of-thailands-caves-99638.

2 James Massola, 'The Thai cave, the monk and the sleeping princess', *Sydney Morning Herald*, 5 July 2018, www.smh.com.au/world/asia/the-thai-cave-the-monk-and-the-sleeping-princess-20180705-p4zpnj.html.

3 Tassanee Vejpongsa and Keweewit Kaewjinda, 'Spirit of mythical princess looms over Thai cave crisis', Khaosod English (website), 28 June 2018, www.khaosodenglish.com/featured/2018/06/28/spirit-of-mythical-princess-looms-over-thai-cave-crisis/.

INTERNATIONAL HELP ARRIVES

1 ABC Four Corners, *Out of the Dark*, www.abc.net.au/4corners/out-of-the-dark/10000580.

2 Channel News Asia, *Against the Elements*, www.channelnewsasia.com/news/video-on-demand/against-the-elements/against-the-elements-10600394.

3 Channel News Asia, *Against the Elements*.

4 About AU$400 to $1200; US$300 to $900.

5 James Massola, 'Birds' nest hunters look for high way out for boys trapped in Thai cave', *Sydney Morning Herald*, 6 July 2018, www.smh.com.au/world/asia/birds-nest-hunters-look-for-high-way-out-for-boys-trapped-in-thai-cave-20180706-p4zpw7.html; AFP, 'Thai

cave rescue: Bird's nest collectors scour for ways into cave to save youth footballers', *Straits Times*, 5 July 2018, www.straitstimes.com/ asia/se-asia/thai-cave-rescue-birds-nest-collectors-scour-for-ways-into-cave-to-save-youth.

6 Piyaporn Wongruang, 'Unknown danger in Thailand's caves', *The Nation*, 21 July 2018, www.nationmultimedia.com/detail/big_read/ 30350523.

FOUND

1 According to the Thai Navy SEALs Facebook page.

2 James Longman, 'Exclusive Thai cave rescue interview: Boys' soccer team, coaches on harrowing experience', ABC News America, 23 August 2018, www.youtube.com/watch?v=Jwo_5UlFwHA&t=2s.

3 *This Morning*, 'The British Divers at the Centre of the Thai Cave Rescue', ITV UK, 16 July 2018, www.youtube.com/watch?v=vdg Bkko1js4.

4 Channel News Asia, *Against the Elements*, www.channelnewsasia. com/news/video-on-demand/against-the-elements/against-the-elements-10600394.

5 James Massola, 'Weather looms as chief danger for Thai cave boys', *Sydney Morning Herald*, 5 July 2018, www.smh.com.au/world/asia/ weather-looms-as-chief-danger-for-thai-cave-boys-20180705-p4zprj.html.

6 Rear Admiral Arpakorn Yuukongkaew, Speech at the Tham Luang cave exhibition, 'Incredible Mission: The Global Agenda', Siam Paragon shopping mall, Bangkok, 23 August 2018.

MESSAGES FROM THE DEEP

1 Rosemary E. Lunn, 'Cave divers Mallinson and Jewel fly out to Thailand', *X-Ray Mag*, 4 July 2018, https://xray-mag.com/content/ cave-divers-mallinson-and-jewel-fly-out-thailand/.

2 ABC Four Corners, *Out of the Dark*, www.abc.net.au/4corners/ out-of-the-dark/10000580.

3   James Massola, '"Don't worry, all fine": Thai boys send letters from the cave', *Sydney Morning Herald*, 7 July 2018, www.smh.com.au/world/asia/don-t-worry-all-fine-thai-boys-send-letters-from-the-cave-20180707-p4zq3w.html?crpt=index.

MISSION CRITICAL

1   James Massola, 'The moment the Thailand cave rescue almost went horribly wrong', *Sydney Morning Herald*, 11 July 2018, www.smh.com.au/world/asia/the-moment-the-thailand-cave-rescue-almost-went-horribly-wrong-20180711-p4zqt5.html.

2   Australian Federal Police, 'Be comfortable being uncomfortable', Platypus: Policing and Community News from the AFP (website), www.afp.gov.au/news-media/platypus/be-comfortable-being-uncomfortable.

3   ABC Four Corners, *Out of the Dark*, www.abc.net.au/4corners/out-of-the-dark/10000580.

4   Josh Zimmerman, 'Thai cave rescue: Perth hero diver Craig Challen speaks on life and death mission', *Perth Now*, 15 July 2018, www.perthnow.com.au/news/wa/thai-cave-rescue-perth-hero-diver-craig-challen-speaks-on-life-and-death-mission-ng-b88895946z.

5   Rear Admiral Arpakorn Yuukongkaew, Speech at the Tham Luang cave exhibition, 'Incredible Mission: The Global Agenda', Siam Paragon shopping mall, Bangkok, 23 August 2018.

SUNDAY, 10.08 AM

1   Josh Zimmerman, 'Thai cave rescue: Perth hero diver Craig Challen speaks on life and death mission', *Perth Now*, 15 July 2018, www.perthnow.com.au/news/wa/thai-cave-rescue-perth-hero-diver-craig-challen-speaks-on-life-and-death-mission-ng-b88895946z.

2   Richard Harris, Speech at the Telstra Vantage conference, Melbourne Convention Centre, 20 September 2018, https://vantage.telstra.com.au/ehome/100180150/agenda.

3   Richard Harris, Q&A at the Swan 2018 Trauma, Critical Care
    and Emergency Surgery Conference, Sheraton on the Park Hotel,
    Sydney, 27 July 2018, http://swanconference.com.

ESCAPE TO FREEDOM

1   Channel Five News UK, 'Thai cave rescue: British diver lost rope
    guide for four minutes during mission' (interview with Chris Jewell),
    18 July 2018, www.youtube.com/watch?v=FM_ooBhvyAc.

2   James Massola and Rachel Clun, 'Thai boys rescued from cave must
    wait to embrace family', *Sydney Morning Herald*, 10 July 2018, www.
    smh.com.au/world/asia/thai-boys-rescued-from-cave-must-wait-
    to-embrace-family-20180710-p4zqio.html?crpt=index.

3   James Massola and Anthony Colangelo, 'Three rescued Thai
    boys have health concerns, the others "fine and normal"', *Sydney
    Morning Herald*, 10 July 2018, www.smh.com.au/world/asia/three-
    rescued-thai-boys-have-health-concerns-the-others-fine-and-
    normal-20180710-p4zqof.html?crpt=index.

MISSION POSSIBLE

1   News.com.au, '"We just couldn't get it to seal': Last perilous
    moments of Thai cave rescue', 28 July 2018, www.news.com.au/
    world/asia/we-just-couldnt-get-it-to-seal-last-perilous-moments-
    of-thai-cave-rescue/news-story/85ad2b9f90e4ccff2d0ce1c6e081
    79a3.

2   Channel Five News UK, 'Thai cave rescue: British diver lost rope
    guide for four minutes during mission' (interview with Chris Jewell),
    18 July 2018, www.youtube.com/watch?v=FM_ooBhvyAc.

3   Australian Federal Police, 'Be comfortable being uncomfortable',
    Platypus: Policing and Community News from the AFP (website),
    www.afp.gov.au/news-media/platypus/be-comfortable-being-
    uncomfortable.

4   Hannah Beech, Richard C. Paddock and Muktita Suhartono,
    '"Still can't believe it worked": The story of the Thai cave rescue',

New York Times, 12 July 2018, www.nytimes.com/2018/07/12/world/asia/thailand-cave-rescue-seals.html.

5 Vaaju.com, 'Kiwi Diver Ross Schnauer details "quite full on" experience during Thai cave rescue', 12 July 2018, https://vaaju.com/newzealand/kiwi-diver-ross-schnauer-details-quite-full-on-experience-during-thai-cave-rescue/.

6 James Massola, 'The moment the Thailand cave rescue almost went horribly wrong', *Sydney Morning Herald*, 11 July 2018, www.smh.com.au/world/asia/the-moment-the-thailand-cave-rescue-almost-went-horribly-wrong-20180711-p4zqt5.html.

EPILOGUE

1 James Massola, Kate Geraghty and Akkarawat Taokwang, '"I can always grow again": Flooded Thai farms count their blessings after cave rescue', *Sydney Morning Herald*, www.smh.com.au/world/asia/i-can-always-grow-again-flooded-thai-farms-count-their-blessings-after-cave-rescue-20180713-p4zrat.html?crpt=index.

2 Rebecca Puddy, Rhett Burnie and Jessica Haynes, 'Take a dive with the Wet Mules', 12 August 2018, ABC Australia, www.abc.net.au/news/2018-08-12/cave-diving-with-the-wet-mules/10090126.